THE
TIGER OF
DRASS

THE
TIGER OF
DRASS

CAPT. ANUJ NAYYAR | 23 |
KARGIL HERO

MEENA NAYYAR AND
HIMMAT SINGH SHEKHAWAT

HarperCollins *Publishers* India

First published in India by HarperCollins *Publishers* 2022
4th Floor, Tower A, Building No. 10, Phase II, DLF Cyber City,
Gurugram, Haryana – 122002
www.harpercollins.co.in

2 4 6 8 10 9 7 5 3

P-ISBN: 978-93-5422-926-8
E-ISBN: 978-93-5422-844-5

Cover design: Saurav Das
Front cover illustration: Mohit Suneja

Typeset in 11.5/15.7 Adobe Garamond at
Manipal Technologies Limited, Manipal

All royalties from the sale of this book will be donated to the families of fallen soldiers.

Printed and bound at
Thomson Press (India) Ltd

 HarperCollinsIn

The Maha Vir Chakra was conferred to Captain Anuj Nayyar at Defence Investiture Ceremony. His father Prof. S.K. Nayyar (left) received the award from President K.R. Narayanan, on 11 April 2000.

Dedicated
to
Prof. S.K. Nayyar

A father, a friend and a mentor to Captain Anuj Nayyar, MVC, he shaped him into the fearless soldier he became in Kargil. His contribution to Anuj's life is as memorable as the story of his brave son.

Wars are fought by nations but won by people. It is but those moments of wisdom that decide which group justifies its cause and is remembered by its people forever. Often, soldiers on either side of the battleline choose to protect their nation's freedom with their lives. Four Param Vir Chakra, ten Maha Vir Chakra, twenty-six Vir Chakra recipients and many other unsung heroes made this choice in the eighty-four days of the battle fought in Kargil in 1999. Captain Anuj Nayyar was awarded the Maha Vir Chakra posthumously for the supreme sacrifice that ensured the victory of his motherland. This account gives you a chance to walk alongside a Maha Vir in the boulder-strewn Drass Valley, engage in combat at an altitude of 17,000 feet, look the enemy in the eye and break bread with fellow soldiers on icy peaks, and kindle a rare patriotism inside you. This book captures Anuj's journey of barely twenty-three years, during which he transformed from a reserved but righteous child to a gem of a military professional. Decades from now, when people celebrate the sovereignty of India and its victories in the battlefield from the time of Independence, Anuj's name will be counted among the bravest of martyrs. Every child will know that he did not succumb to age, that he ran out of breath and not courage, that he looked death in the eye and decided to trade his life for the invaluable freedom of his land. This is the epic saga of Captain Anuj Nayyar, MVC, the Tiger of Drass.

Contents

Foreword

A WAR IS THE ULTIMATE test for armies and their soldiers. Victory in war is achieved because battles are won. The war in Kargil will go down in military history as a saga of unmatched bravery, grit and determination. Most of the credit for the victory in Kargil goes to the bravery and dedication of young officers and soldiers. They were up front, not hesitant to make any sacrifice to uphold the regimental and national pride and dignity. Under their brilliant leadership, our troops performed superbly. There were countless acts of gallantry, displays of steely resilience, single-minded devotion to duty and tremendous sacrifices. Captain Anuj Nayyar of 17 Jat Battalion left one such mark.

During the 1999 Kargil war, Pakistan Army had occupied Point 4875 and the ridge line leading to it from the west of Tiger Hill. This height dominated the road from Zoji La to Drass. Tactically, this objective was almost as important as Tololing. HQ 8 Mountain Division made the plan to recapture Point 4875, a large and spread-out objective, as soon as a major part of its artillery was free after capturing Tiger Hill. The main objective, that is, Point 4875, was divided into several parts – Pimple 1, Whale Back, Pimple 2 and then the height Point 4875.

17 Jat was asked to recapture Pimple 1, Whale Back and Pimple 2. The battalion launched its attack on 4 July 1999. Capt. Anuj Nayyar was part of the 'C' company, which was tasked to capture Pimple 2 in the second phase of the attack. While moving towards the objective, the company commander was seriously injured and had to be evacuated. Without a murmur, like a good second-in-command, young Anuj took over the C company. This gallant officer, highly motivated and determined to achieve success for his company, decided to lead the assault personally. After he and his men had cleared three enemy sangars, eliminated nine soldiers and were in the process of clearing the fourth bunker, an enemy rocket-propelled grenade hit him directly. However, by then, the intrepid young officer had discharged his huge responsibility in an exemplary manner. In doing so, he made the supreme sacrifice for his country.

Anuj had shown a great sense of responsibility and extreme courage in the face of the enemy. Despite the difficult circumstances, he led his company from the front. His courage and leadership became a great inspiration to his troops. This impact can best be gauged when one of his fellow soldiers, Tejbir Singh, decided to name his son after Anuj.

For his indomitable resolve, grit and determination, and for motivating his command by personal example, young Anuj had acted well beyond the call of duty. He was awarded the nation's second highest gallantry award, the Maha Vir Chakra. Soon after his sacrifice, my wife and I went over to convey our condolences to Anuj's parents who lived in Janakpuri at the time. That was one of the saddest duties I performed being the head of our great organization, the Indian Army.

General V.P. Malik (Retd)
PVSM, AVSM
Former Chief of the Army Staff

~~~

Never Say Die

The battle cry of the Jat Regiment – 'Jat Balwan, Jai Bhagwan' – echoed in the Mushkoh Valley on the fateful night of July 1999, when the brave and determined troops of 17 Jat, led from the front by Capt. Anuj Nayyar in one of the bloodiest battles of the Kargil war, captured the heights occupied by enemy troops. Young Anuj, in the highest tradition of the Indian Army, laid down his life but ensured that the name of 17 Jat and his tale of valour became legendary in his regiment and the armed forces. One of the youngest recipients of the Maha Vir Chakra, Anuj has left a legacy that inspires not just his unit but the entire Jat Regiment.

As colonel of the Jat Regiment, I had visited Anuj's unit. Memories of him and other braves of the unit who had made the supreme sacrifice during this battle are well preserved in the Hall of Fame, which is the first stop for all newly posted officers and men in the unit.

The Tiger of Drass is a collaborative effort by Anuj's mother Meena Nayyar and Himmat Singh Shekhawat based on interviews with officers and men of 17 Jat who were then part of the battalion, with inputs available in open source. Mrs Nayyar has also pieced together the letters and memories of Anuj that will bring to the fore the never before known facets of the young officer's personality. I deeply appreciate their efforts in bringing one of the legendary figures of the Kargil war to life.

Lt Gen. S.K. Saini
PVSM, AVSM, YSM, VSM, ADC
Vice Chief of the Army Staff

'And how can man die better
  Than facing fearful odds.
For the ashes of his fathers.
  And the temples of his gods'

– From the poem 'Horatius',
by Thomas Babington Macaulay

While twenty-one years have passed since the war in Kargil, the memory of those who lost their lives in response to the perfidious actions of an enemy can never die. The battles were fought in the most inhospitable terrains of the world, at heights ranging from 14 –18,000 feet. One such battle which brought a closure to the war was fought on the icy heights of Point 4875 by 17 Jat led by Col. Umesh Bawa, which was part of the 79 Mountain Brigade.

By mid-day of 5 July, Point 4875 had been captured, though important features like Pimple 2 were still with the enemy. The second phase of the attack was launched on the night 5 and 6 July, with the Charlie Company tasked to capture Pimple 2. During the attack, Anuj's company commander was wounded and the command of the company devolved on his young shoulders. The enemy was engaging the attacking troops with artillery and mortar fire. Undeterred by the heavy fire, Anuj led his troops and pressed home the attack, and succeeded in capturing a major portion of the objective. While the remnant bunkers were being attacked, an enemy RPG directed towards Anuj killed him instantly. However, his actions contributed in sealing the fate of the enemy in the Mushkoh Valley and a grateful Indian Army and the nation conferred the country's second highest bravery award on Anuj Nayyar.

Anuj was an enthusiastic young officer and I had the honour of meeting him a couple of times. On the battlefield he displayed courage, bravery and determination to achieve the task entrusted to him, going beyond the call of duty and sacrificing his life so that we all could have a better tomorrow. This is what legends are made of, and I salute his mother Mrs Nayyar in keeping his memory alive and facing her personal loss with dignity and pride.

Lt Gen. Mohinder Puri (Retd)
PVSM, UYSM
Former Commander of 8 Mountain Division &
Deputy Chief of the Army Staff

A Stellar Tale of Passion and Courage

Capt. Anuj Nayyar, MVC, was a warrior par excellence, a braveheart who exemplified selflessness, frontline leadership and tactical acumen far beyond his two years of service. Commissioned into 17 Jat in

June 1997, he saw active service in the Kashmir Valley with his unit in his initial years. But in June 1999, when Pakistan attempted to wrest the Kargil heights from the Indian Army, his unit was inducted into the Mushkoh sector to evict the intruders. Pakistani presence at the heights of 16–17,000 feet created a potential threat to the crucial Zoji La pass which connected the cities of Srinagar, Kargil and Leh.

Through this brief I wish to highlight the enormity of Capt. Anuj Nayyar's contribution to the battle in Mushkoh and also the degree of difficulty he faced in executing the task. The 17 Jat was tasked to secure Pimple 2, a peak within the Pimple Complex, on the western slopes of the 16,000-feet-high Point 4875. Well coordinated and mutually supporting automatic fire from the pinnacle and the spurs prevented upward movement, with interference in all attempts to even capture any of the spurs. Capt. Nayyar's company was tasked to attack the objective without softening through precision airstrikes and limited artillery. Even before the assault could begin his company commander was injured, leaving the command of 100-odd men on the young shoulders of Capt. Nayyar. Directing junior commissioned officers and men much more experienced than him, getting them to accept the risk of assaulting and destroying bunkers, overpowering the enemy who seemed innumerable and ensuring least casualties on his side became his responsibility. Capt. Nayyar's passion, courage and ability to adapt to the situation got the men of his company to follow him. He was there, right in front in each such assault, adrenaline flowing and his youthful spirit sparking fire in his men. Ordinarily an officer casualty at the beginning of an operation shatters morale because it takes time to build trust between the leader and the led. In this case, the men knew Capt. Nayyar and his energetic personality but not his fearlessness under the heaviest odds. Seeing their officiating commander moving without any concern for his personal safety fired their spirits too and the company delivered the objective. The destruction of three enemy bunkers was attributed to Capt. Nayyar, as also the death of at least nine Pakistani soldiers; a superhuman effort by someone so young and inexperienced. His professional acumen can be judged by the fact that he destroyed these bunkers in copybook style, employing rocket launchers from a flank and then assaulting each of them. The warriors who transform themselves into super beings in hours of crisis are remembered forever.

Capt. Nayyar's revered mother invited me to write a short description of her warrior son. I could find no better dedication to the young warrior than the sheer description of what involves an assault in the mountains. Her braveheart son immortalized himself through his courage and leadership. He was conferred the second highest gallantry award of the nation. Yet the greatest recognition remains the memories that his troops carry of his selfless action, taking upon himself as much danger as his soldiers did. That recognition is beyond words and awards. Capt. Anuj Nayyar, MVC (P), rest in peace. A grateful nation thanks you.

Lt Gen. Syed Ata Hasnain (Retd)
PVSM, UYSM, AVSM, SM, VSM (Bar)
Former Commander of 15 Army Corps &
Millitary Secretary of the Indian Army

One for All, All for One

Captain Anuj Nayyar was commissioned into the 17th Battalion of the Jat Regiment in June 1997. I was extremely happy to get an ex-NDA officer from Delhi commissioned into our battalion because I, too, was an ex-NDA from Delhi. He was a youngster full of energy, and always ready to take on additional responsibilities with a smile. He was physically fit and fond of sports. I had seen him rubbing shoulders with colleagues in the volleyball court. Soon, he became popular among them for his do-or-die quality.

As a young leader, he was humble, fair and honest in his dealings. He was confident and loyal to both superiors and soldiers. He was always willing to bat for the soldiers and willing to defend them. He had built a rapport with his men by respecting them regardless of their rank. These qualities made him a popular leader amongst them who were ready to do whatever he asked. This was the reason behind the victory Capt. Nayyar and his company achieved during the Kargil war.

Before the war, when I promoted Nayyar to the rank of captain, I told him, 'With each star added to your shoulders, your responsibilities towards your men increase. I am confident that you will live up to the addition responsibilities thrust upon you.' I can now vouch with confidence that he lived up to his reputation and commitment far beyond my imagination.

During the attack on Pimple 2, the C company commander got injured in enemy fire and the responsibility to lead the company fell on Capt. Nayyar's shoulders. Without hesitation he took control over the situation and led his company in assault with the determination of a tiger. Seeing his confidence, his men also followed him into battle. He led by example. In the process, he killed nine enemy soldiers and destroyed three enemy sangars. While leading his men to the capture of the fourth sangar, Capt. Nayyar was hit on the right shoulder by a freak rocket projectile, which killed him on the spot.

Capt. Nayyar was awarded the Maha Vir Chakra for the gallantry he displayed in the battle of the Pimple Complex. I think he deserved the highest honour, the Param Vir Chakra. The battalion earned a unit citation, a battle honour for Mushkoh and a theatre honour for its contribution in Kargil. Capt. Nayyar became one of the 'Mushkoh warriors', of which we are proud.

His story of valour is narrated to young soldiers and officers who join the unit. He has left an indelible mark on his unit, regiment and the Indian Army. This book is a recognition of his leadership qualities, which will inspire generations.

I, as his commanding officer in war, continue to live with the guilt that I was not able to bring back Anuj safely to his parents. I owe my sincere apology to them. Jai Hind.

Brig. Umesh Singh Bawa (Retd), VrC, SM
Former Commanding Officer, 17 Jat

Braveheart Anuj

In the summer of 1999, as a twenty-four-year-old journalist, I was among the first into the Kargil war zone, a fledgling reporter in the middle of one of the most intense situations anyone could imagine.

Death was all around. You could see it. If you looked up at the blue skies, you would often see artillery shells as they flew past. If you actually saw these shells, you knew you were safe. The ones that may have had your name on them were the ones that you occasionally heard. A shrill whistling sound. The louder it was, the closer it was to where you were.

Early one morning, we left our hotel in Kargil to report. When we returned, a part of the same hotel had been struck. All around us, there were signs of a great Indian fight back. The enemy had to be thrown out of our territory, at any cost.

India had a new band of heroes – twenty-something soldiers – young lieutenants, captains and majors who would lead the charge up the barren mountain sides in the face of relentless enemy gunfire. They would engage in unprecedented mountain warfare – some of the most intense infantry duels since the Second World War.

Capt. Anuj Nayyar, almost exactly a year younger than me, was one of the bravehearts who charged up those hill-sides, among his first targets – securing Pimple 2, on Point 4875 in the Mushkoh Valley. During the initial phase of the assault, Capt. Nayyar's company commander was injured. Command of the operation now rested on the shoulders of the twenty-three-year-old. Moving forward in the face of intense artillery shelling and mortar fire, he destroyed an enemy bunker, fighting with his men at an altitude of 15,590 feet. Moving from bunker to bunker, Nayyar and his men killed nine Pakistani soldiers and destroyed three machine gun nests. But then, in the flash of a second, the young captain was hit – killed by an enemy rocket-propelled grenade. He died instantly. When it was all over, forty-six Pakistani soldiers lay dead. With them, eleven of India's bravest.

One of them was Capt. Nayyar. The mission that he was a part of was among the toughest imaginable. He carried on his duty with resolve and determination, leading his men from the front in the face of overwhelming adversity.

The young captain was indomitable – a true infantry soldier and a young leader. Motivated and fearless, he was part of a band of brothers who liberated a part of India in the summer of 1999.

Vishnu Som
Senior Editor and Principal Anchor, NDTV

1

The Beginning

My army and this country have put so much faith in me; it would be a mistake to think of death at this time. Till the last enemy is not defeated, I will keep breathing.

— Capt. Anuj Nayyar, MVC

'MANI, I'VE CLEARED THE NDA exam and I might receive my SSB call soon,' Anuj announced to his mother on his way to a volleyball game. He did not feel the need to explain, or wait for a reaction. The seventeen-year-old was gone in a blink. He was, of course, referring to the prestigious National Defence Academy examination for joining the Indian armed forces which the teenager had passed.

Days went by but Anuj did not receive a call letter from the Service Selection Board, a body that assesses a candidate's suitability for becoming an officer in the armed forces. Mani, a name fondly used by Anuj and his younger brother Karan for their mother, had started growing restless. That's when Prof. Nayyar – Poppin to his sons, Mani's husband and the hero of the family – stepped in. Instead of waiting for an intimation, the professor decided to approach the corresponding army office for information.

An excited Anuj learnt that he had to report to the Allahabad Service Selection Board the following day. His father accompanied him to Allahabad Junction, where army officials waited to escort Anuj and other candidates to the selection centre. As the son waited for his turn before the selection board, the father recalled his own experience of being interviewed for the Indian Air Force when he, too, was seventeen.

A man for whom the love of his country was nothing short of a religion, the professor had not, until then, disclosed details of his own interview to the family. As they waited for word on Anuj's fate, Poppin reminisced about his time before the selection panel.

He did not make it to the final list even though he had cleared the psychological and intelligence trials. When asked what he would do if he were in enemy territory with a bad weapons system and insufficient fuel for return to base, he said he would take down the target by crash-landing his plane.

Some soldiers are born to do their country's bidding, some are born to die for it; for Poppin, it was being one with the nation. The country lives through its soldiers, who uphold the nation's security and honour in every situation – the same thought that guided Anuj through his attack on the enemy in Kargil and helped him accomplish his duties without worrying about consequences.

Prof. Nayyar waited at the Allahabad station until the army officials came for Anuj. Before leaving, Anuj reached for his father and held him close before saying, 'I am going to make it, Poppin. I promise you.' His father did not say a word; he only grasped his son tighter as the duo quietly bid farewell.

Anuj went with the officials without once turning back. Parents often linger in the hope that their children, while entering a new phase of their life, will look back at least once. But Anuj did not. Neither at the Allahabad station that day nor while charging up the hills of Drass a few years later.

Poppin stood still as he watched his firstborn disappear into the crowd at the end of the platform. It was a moment of truth for the professor as he realized the magnitude of his son's career choice. Before emotions overwhelmed him, he sat down on the steps of an overbridge. It took the father only a minute to make peace with his son's decision. 'He's off to his destiny now,' he said to himself. Prof. Nayyar had officially handed his son over to the nation.

For his part, Anuj was not just a soldier who was true to his duty and country. He always did more than was expected of him. That's what he did that fateful night in 1999, at the Drass sector during Operation Vijay. He laid the foundation of India's victory in exchange for his own life.

But Anuj was not always the fearless fighter. He was a quiet, docile child. His is the story of continuous transition – from a calm and composed boy to a rebellious lad, from a passionate athlete to a responsible cadet, from a duty-bound soldier to a respectful officer and from a valiant platoon commander to a martyr.

Kargil saw many such symbols of transformation in 1999. With every such story, the mountains that stood witness, too, changed forever. Every rock that Anuj might have rested on must have felt the strength of his resolve; every stone he crushed under his feet must have endured his physical mettle; every surface he touched must have felt the tenderness in his heart for his loved ones. This is the story of how a young Anuj became the Maha Vir Chakra

Captain Anuj Nayyar. This is a story of his journey–from 28 August 1975 to 7 July 1999, and beyond.

~~~

Born to Fight

Anuj was not due till 4 September 1975 but he chose to come into the world early. He arrived at 10.14 a.m., on 28 August. To Mani, a new mother, her bundle of joy was an exact replica of herself. But it seemed that the newborn held a secret deep within. 'The Nayyar part was more predominant in him than the Dhingra side (Mani's maiden name),' in the mother's own words.

Anuj's s bravery and confidence came from his father while his clarity of thought and thirst for knowledge were inherited from his mother. Appearance wise, too, the boy was a mix of his parents: he had his father's build and his mother's features. With time, the Delhi boy started to imbibe other qualities from his parents. He displayed a cool fearlessness under the most trying circumstances, à la his father. His organizational skills and honesty came from his mother. All in all, a neat little package of skills and values that distinguished him from many others of his age.

Anuj's tryst with adversities began right after birth. He was born healthy at a nursing home in West Delhi's Rajouri Garden area. But soon his health declined and so did his weight. The boy, however, was up for a fight. Mani wonders if Anuj would have been a different person if he were not born on that day. But it seems that soldiers born on 28 August are destined to be immortals.

~~~

The Smiling Rebel: Anuj's Childhood

Janakpuri, a residential area in West Delhi, was the castle of this prince who was born into a wholesome family of elder cousins, paternal uncles, grandparents and other relatives. Soon he was blessed with a baby brother – Karan. Karan and cousin Tina were the loves of his life while Ashish, an elder cousin, was his comrade in arms. Life was simple back then – it was all about mischief with the siblings, weekend trips to India Gate on the Vespa, sweets and balloons and dinners at Embassy Restaurant, Connaught Place.

Anuj's life revolved around his father, and he hung on to his every word – even if it meant listening to the same breakfast story daily – and picked up his hobbies too.

Karan was the centre of his small world. He protected him in the way a father guards his son. Anuj would carry him on his back on holiday trips, push his toy jeep through the streets, and even step in to solve quarrels between Karan and his friends in school. That's where the sense of brotherhood with the unit came from. His classmates, his platoon mates, even co-ops officers commended his ability to find a connection with everyone. Not a visibly mushy and emotional bond, but an honourable, everlasting connection that anyone could call to test at any moment in life.

Coming to terms with injustice or dishonesty was alien to Anuj's nature. He could not even stomach attempts at cheating by his grandfather during a game of carrom at home!

A quiet, simple Anuj, whom no one ever imagined in roles of absolute defiance, changed after his childhood years. The unrest within, the questions that he kept to himself, pushing against the walls of conscience, found the key to liberation. Flashes of this change came to the fore under different circumstances. Once, during a game of volleyball in school, he stood up to a senior who was flouting the rules. Within minutes he was surrounded by seniors who wanted to rough him up. He was outnumbered, but not outwitted. He made it home, safe and sound, but a changed person. That day he promised to lead a life of principles and exemplary physical fitness.

———

From a close-knit joint family to a household of just four – the Nayyars entered another phase of their life when they moved into a smaller flat in 1986. Anuj was about eleven years old then. Along with a new address, the family also adapted to new routines, responsibilities and environment. Anuj's personality benefited from the ambience of open thinking, which was decidedly different from the more homely and conservative joint family structure. At the same time, the boy acquired a greater understanding of his duties and values as a son, brother and human being. He developed a strong dislike for abusive behaviour – in language, action or thought. He lived by his rules and values as passionately as he followed Poppin's lessons on science and mathematics. The father, who recorded lessons for his sons on the tape recorder every night, also inspired them to acknowledge and respect a woman's place in the family. The black granite name plate outside the flat read: *Ghar Meena ka*, or Meena's house. At home, the rule of thumb was 'Mani is always right'. All three male members of this Janakpuri household followed this like gospel. If the boys ever found the father in an argument with Mani, they would step in to remind him of the rule that he himself had set. The nudge always worked like magic. Well, almost always, except once when the professor, eager to establish his lordship over the study room, pasted a piece of paper next to the nameplate of the house. The revised text read thus: *Ghar Meena ka, ek kamra pati ka*, or Meena's house, one room belongs to the husband.

Anuj's commitment to routine and discipline was uncommon. As the older brother, he was always eager to have Karan do the same. He would not let the youngest Nayyar slip even when Mani was recovering from a serious illness at the hospital. 'He didn't want Karan to take advantage of my absence,' recalls the mother. Once, when the boys were visiting her at the hospital, Mani noticed a tear in Karan's eye. Something told her that it had to do with Anuj, the unflinching disciplinarian. It turned out that he had scolded Karan for not having his dinner on time. 'I had to do something to make him go to bed before Poppin came home,' said Anuj. 'Karan has to learn to follow the schedule.' These were the words of a brother who not only looked after his sibling but also disciplined him. But the importance of rules and routine were never enforced through physical punishment. Anuj never raised a hand on Karan. The latter, out of respect, never talked back or misbehaved.

Anuj's strength of character did not come from values alone. It also drew from his love of sports – volleyball, especially – and physical fitness. He would not walk when he could run. He liked to work his limbs while running errands. When he was in high school, he dropped Karan to school even on days when he was on leave. One morning, after his bike broke down in Janakpuri, Anuj dragged Karan by the wrist and made him run all the way, about twelve kilometres, to his school in Dhaula Kuan. Karan did not have an exam that day nor any assembly function to perform at, but being late to school – or anywhere for that matter – was unimaginable to Anuj. They made it in time, Karan recalls. 'That day, he also decided that I needed more practice in running.' Thus began a new regimen for the youngest Nayyar.

A Wise Head on Young Shoulders

Prof. Nayyar would often organize inter-society sports competitions where his sons made him proud. Anuj's enthusiasm for sports made him sparkle on the field. He inspired children in his neighbourhood just as he did the soldiers in the treacherous terrain of Drass. It was not the feat an average company, nor even a well-trained Ghatak Unit (counter-insurgency tactical units of the Indian Army), could achieve easily – but Anuj and his men outdid themselves.

Sports and fitness were two constants in Anuj's life. Playing volleyball in school, running at NDA, boxing and combat training at the Indian Military Academy (IMA) and life with his battalion added to the person he was. Every time he challenged himself, he made sure that the finishing line was not easy to conquer. It was his way of keeping himself from becoming complacent.

As a child, physical training was Anuj's opportunity to get to know his father and develop a friendship with him. For the professor, it was a chance to learn about the new generation. They shared a love for branded sports shoes and photography equipment. Anuj even managed to get his father to buy him an air gun. The fascination for arms and combat runs in the family, thanks to Anuj's grandfather Lieutenant Bakshi Ram Nayyar, a veteran of the Second World War. The rooftop of the Janakpuri apartment building is where Anuj got his first lessons in using the air gun under his father's close supervision, who was by then a willing accomplice to his son's adventures.

These training sessions would often lead to complaints from neighbours who were hassled by the noise. Anuj, however, always managed to pacify them. He would either smile through the interaction or reason with the complainant. At NDA, too, Anuj used his smile to appease seniors on whom he played pranks.

As a child, Anuj liked to handle complaints or disagreements by himself, without running to his parents for advice or support. He stayed calm and courteous even in the face of a barrage of complaints. Once when a neighbouring family came home to accuse Anuj of roughing up their son, he did not utter a single word. Only after they had left and Mani questioned him did he say it was silly of the boy to trouble his parents over a trivial matter. Mani did not understand him then. After all, Anuj was mature beyond his years.

Not the Quiet One

Calm and composed Anuj also had his moments of rage, especially when his protective side was triggered. When Tina, his beloved cousin, sought his help in thwarting the advances of a boy, Anuj first advised her to ignore him. Anuj always maintained that everyone should take the first step towards solving problems on their own. He liked to watch over from a distance, choosing to step in only when things appeared to worsen or got out of hand. This is how he approached Tina's problem as well. But the besotted boy in question continued to bother Tina and she brought up the matter to Ashish and Anuj, her brothers and guardian angels.

Anuj asked Tina to fix a meeting with the boy. The plan was to have a quiet, one-on-one chat with him. Things were going according to the plan – Anuj took him to a corner of the school ground. But he flew off the handle when the boy made a lewd remark about Tina. When Ashish reached the spot – he was keeping an eye on the two from a distance – Anuj was holding the delinquent upside down. He did not hit the boy or abuse him, but he made sure he would think twice about harassing anyone again.

Anuj's anger was always triggered by actions that challenged the values of honour, respect and humanity. It was the same with the intruders in Kargil. He did not have malice in his heart for any country but the sight of the bodies of dead soldiers being airlifted from the conflict zone drove his resolve of paying back with the same coin.

The army looks for personality traits among recruits that it describes as 'officer-like qualities' or OLQs. It maps certain qualities while selecting cadets for any programme and hones the OLQs via training. According to Mani, Anuj had OLQs such as a sense of duty even in his early teens. From protecting his cousin from harassment to standing up for a friend who was beaten up by bullies in school – and getting him first-aid – Anuj had displayed esprit de corps time and again.

He was a soldier, a hero, even before he left home to join the armed forces and build a legacy of his own.

~

Out of the Cocoon and into the Den

'Nayyar sahab, I can't take this any longer.' Anuj's mathematics teacher in school was in a flap. He held his hands out and asked the professor to check his pulse. 'This lad of yours is never in class. He is either playing volleyball or roaming around with his cousin Ashish,' he added. 'I'm worried he might fail.' The father heard it all but knew that his son was not made for failure. Anuj would never repeat a class.

Anuj had a knack for defeating the odds. Once, while fixing the lights at a volleyball court, he accidentally touched a live wire. It stuck to his hand for a few moments till Ashish managed to unplug it from the main switchboard. Anuj was in a lot of pain but he overcame it.

'Pain is in the mind. If you don't feel it, you don't get hurt by it.' He lived by this belief. It became clear when he met with a scooter accident at the age of seventeen. Then, too, Ashish was him. They managed to hide the injury from the family till Mani stumbled upon Anuj's blood-soaked shoe. He was immediately rushed to a hospital where he decided to undergo treatment – skin grafting – without anaesthesia. His mother believes that it was a litmus test he had set for himself because he wanted to see if he was suited for a career in the armed forces.

The injury and the recovery time gave Anuj the break he needed to prepare for the NDA entrance exam. This is when he developed a special bond with the encyclopaedias and journals that his father was so fond of collecting. He pored over these as he opened his mind to gaining practical knowledge through deduction, dissection and logic.

Once he cleared the exam, Anuj showed little interest in school. This bothered his parents who were worried that he would fail his board exams. 'He still needed the cut-off marks or 33 per cent in his boards to be able to join the NDA,' Mani says, but Anuj showed no signs of seriousness. Finally, his father had to sit him down and lecture him on the discipline he needed to bring back in his daily routine.

Anuj finally made peace with his untamed enthusiasm and concentrated on his studies. He secured 65 per cent in the exams.

He jumped out of his bed to hug his delighted parents when they informed him about his results.

During his last days at the Army Public School, Dhaula Kuan, the school unveiled its yearbook. The book referred to Anuj as 'lethal weapon'. It seemed an appropriate moniker for a student whose father was a regular at the principal's office and whose teachers lost sleep over the mischief he made. Anuj was the student who liked to enjoy his tiffin during the Monday unit tests and use the exam sheets to wipe his mouth.

Anuj was also popular among the girls in his school. Many of them had a crush on him and sent him romantic cards and letters. He enjoyed the attention but never let it get to his head. His fiancée Timmie was among the girls who liked the dashing teen. He, too, liked Timmie but the nature of their friendship changed only after he joined the defence academy, the base he aspired for.

Anuj's past held him in good stead at the NDA. He still stood up for what was right, he still had the smile that could melt rocks, and he was still the maverick at heart. The soldier who conquered the mountains of Drass during the Kargil war was a combination of learnings he had absorbed over his young years.

'Leave the enemy to god's mercy; they will get their justice,' Anuj said on the ascent to the post on Pimple 2. 'But let us make arrangements for the enemy to meet his god in the first place,' he concluded.

2

Through the Pastures of Destiny

I have enhanced my skills in the art of fighting with weapons, knives and my bare hands. The day will never come when I admit defeat.

– Capt. Anuj Nayyar, MVC

ANUJ'S FIRST DAY AT the National Defence Academy was rather eventful.

In his head and heart, Anuj was already a member of the Indian Army. The Army Public School in Delhi was a stepping stone towards this love. He had schooled both his body and mind for the armed forces. And he was prepared to not let anyone dampen his enthusiasm as he set foot in the hallowed halls of the academy. The welcome, however, was unusual.

He was in the second batch to report to the academy. By the time he walked in to register as a cadet, others in the first batch had been brought down a couple of notches – from the initial heady rush of making it to the National Defence Academy – with a mandatory crew cut and an official briefing on rules, routines, etiquette, discipline and decorum. Anuj was yet to be 'treated' when he entered the classroom with long hair and sunglasses.

The senior cadet who was leading the orientation that day was as baffled as the freshers. 'Where are you from?' he asked.

His backpack slung over his shoulders, Anuj replied, 'Delhi.'

No salutation, no courtesy. Only the answer.

The class had just been briefed on official courtesy and forms of address. Anuj was in clear violation of both. The senior cadet would not let him off so easily. 'Don't you know that you have to use "sir" while addressing a senior?' he charged at Anuj.

The newcomer shot back immediately, 'I have only reported here, not joined yet.'

Never a fan of norms, Anuj had his way of dealing with situations, awkward and otherwise. His way may not have always pleased everyone but it was always more thrilling or exciting. Anuj's first interaction with the senior cadet helped his batchmate Col. Ashok Thakur make up his mind about one thing. He could either brand the Delhi lad arrogant and avoid him, or he could become his friend and admire the leader and comrade in him. He chose the second option.

It would not be wrong to say that a person who goes to the NDA becomes the NDA. Every cadet grows his roots at Sudan Hall, the administration building; daily routines become a religion in the institute that accepts them wholeheartedly and sends them back into the world as beacons of excellence. For Anuj, the place was more than that. It was home turf for the lad who had been brought up on NDA ideals by his father.

'While others struggled with drills and the physical rigours, this guy was enjoying every bit of what the academy had to offer,' recalls Col. Thakur, who was also his course-mate.

At the time, the NDA housed over 2,000 cadets in fifteen squadrons every academic year. 'Anuj and I were part of the Echo Squadron of 1993–96 batch, which was the ninetieth batch of the squadron, or what we used to call the 'eagle squadron'. So, as a combination of the Echo Squadron's timeline and the names we came up with for our batch, we chose to call ourselves '90 Echelons,' says Col. Thakur. In his words, Anuj remained a '90 Echelon for the rest of his life. Little did he know that his legacy would become a part of what NDA cadets are now taught in class – in the same halls where Col. Thakur and he tried to stay awake after a tiring drill, exchanged notes and laid the foundation of an undying friendship.

The place held a certain charm for Anuj. Discipline, fitness and fidelity, the three main ideals of the academy, were wired in him. That made it easy for him to become conspicuous among a sea of fresh cadets from both India and countries with which it has friendly relations. Anuj did not speak a lot, recalls Col. Thakur, but he still had what is commonly referred to as people skills. 'He didn't speak out of turn, or in an indiscreet manner, and yet he generated a certain curiosity around him,' says the former course-mate. 'Most of us would keep wondering "what's Anuj going to do now" or "how is he going to handle this task or exercise",' he adds.

Where a cadet takes an average of three to four weeks to acquaint himself with the NDA regime, Anuj took only three to four days to find his rhythm. This was remarkable for a person who, like most of his batchmates, was away from home for the first time, and finding his feet to become self-reliance. The rigorous selection process filters out people who are unlikely to survive the NDA. Anuj did not just survive the academy, he imbibed it.

During '*ragda*', NDA's version of the ragging that students face in civilian institutes, Anuj's smile helped him win the admiration of both his batchmates and seniors.

Anuj went through each task with confidence. He took only a few minutes to switch from one uniform to another (NDA has nine uniforms for cadets). He would do more push-ups and crunches than the number asked of him. And he would never say no to extra exercise and physical challenges. He just smiled.

The tactic worked. Everyone agreed that this cadet was not to be taken lightly.

Anuj had some former students from his Delhi school among his seniors at the academy. Some of them had an axe to grind with the young Nayyar, thanks to his adventures in the higher secondary years. Anuj, however, was unafraid of the consequences of having a senior with a grudge against him at the academy, or a battalion for that matter. He did not express regret for decisions that pitted him against some of his seniors in school. 'His principles were cast in stone,' says Col. Thakur. This paid off in the long run. It turned school-time rivalry and grudges into friendships born out of mutual respect and trust.

An NDA graduate, after training for three years, usually takes twelve months to clear the Indian Military Academy (IMA). And what he learns and assimilates at the NDA propels him through the subsequent stages of training, specialization and service. It is common to find officers of the Indian Army falling back upon the learnings of their cadet training days, and not just for professional reasons. They also cherish the academy for the camaraderie with fellow cadets. With time, NDA graduates acquire new titles as officers, some even bag medals and decorations for excellence in the field. But perhaps none is so dear to them as the nicknames and the identity acquired during the NDA days.

When Anuj confronted adversaries in Drass and conquered the Pimples, he was a soldier with multiple identities: Division Cadet Captain Anuj Nayyar, Echo Squadron, NDA 1996; Gentleman Cadet Anuj Nayyar, Naushera Company, Cariappa Battalion, IMA 1997; and Captain Anuj Nayyar, Charlie Company, 17 Jat Battalion, Indian Army 1999. In his heart, however, he was a proud '90 Echelon.

~~~

A Soldier in the Making

The NDA is the gateway to the armed forces. And its cadets the future of defence. They are schooled in a wide array of subjects and fields: from the sciences to physical fitness, from tactical studies to foundation courses in desired specializations. It goes without saying, the curriculum includes a combination of athletics and studies; almost all of it is held outdoors. Anuj's father held that the world outside had more to teach than any classroom or laboratory. This helped the man shake off occasional complaints regarding Anuj's performance from the teachers in his school. He knew that his son had found the perfect setting at NDA which nurtured both his physical and academic selves.

'Anuj was a model student for the NDA. He was already an athlete when he got into the academy. While many struggled to do twenty-five sets of front rolls and short sprints, he was able to do eighty to a hundred with ease,' says Col. Thakur. Esprit de corps was not something that he imbibed from his time at the NDA; instead, he inspired many to perfect this characteristic there. Anuj was an embodiment of the perfect officer with all the requisite officer-like qualities.

One thing he was not happy about was his somewhat average running speed. Despite being good at it in school, he was still behind some cadets at the academy.

So Anuj squeezed out time for practice from NDA's hectic daily routine. Out of the two daily physical training sessions and a sports session, he came up with his own version of a training module for running. He included his batchmates in the sessions as well, and practised cross-country runs and volleyball with them. Anuj loathed stagnancy. It seemed that he was always raring to cross the levels of the game called life.

He had a fun side too; most of his NDA mates remember him for being the quirky one in sticky situations. Anuj used to eagerly wait for the NDA camps where squadrons took part in collaborative exercises, joint outdoor missions and training sessions. These camps also provided bonding time for cross-border cadets, cadets from different regions and walks of life.

Camp Greenhorn is the first outdoor camp for newly inducted cadets. It is called Greenhorn because the cadets are exposed for the first time to the vagaries and rigours of military life, in a packed week full of tasks such as long route marches with battle load, night navigation, and preparation of defences in open mountains and even jungles. Among other exercises such as night navigation, adaptive training and circuit training, there was one programme that needed participants to be awake for ninety-six hours straight and complete certain exercises within the time frame. 'We were asked to dig a tactical trench, which resembles a pit for the ground post of weapons units,' says Col. Thakur.

The instruction to dig the trench was given on the third day of the camp, at 10 p.m. sharp. The weary cadets, getting a taste of the life they had chosen, were somewhere between the states of drowsiness and wakefulness. According to Col. Thakur, 'Most of them thought the digging exercise would finally break them.' Anuj, however, continued to smile and dig.

'One by one, the cadets fell like dominoes in the trench, but there was no stopping Anuj,' Col. Thakur recalls. 'He said, "Now that we have taken this up, let us at least make it look like we made a credible effort," and kept at the task.'

After digging a five-foot-deep trench, Anuj and a few others decided to catch forty winks. Instead of falling asleep in the trench, Anuj suggested that they look for a spot in the bushes nearby. And as a ploy to escape a surprise inspection by the training captain, he arranged some of the helmets on the edge of the pit. He hoped that in the pre-dawn light, it would appear as though the cadets were still at work inside the trench. Close to four in the morning, a sharp cry from the trench jolted the cadets out of their sleep. The training officer, familiar with every trick in the book, had come checking on the group. He decided to wake the cadets by hitting the helmets with the butt of his rifle. It was a blow strong enough to rattle every person in the vicinity – particularly the hapless cadet who was actually wearing the helmet and napping in the pit.

The cry was a warning call for the cadets who immediately crawled back into the trench. Upon inspection, the training officers appreciated the work of the group. After the camp, the cadets had a good laugh over the helmet trick.

Even today, Anuj's batchmates recall how he inspired them to be better people, not just good officers. Differences of opinion with a person did not count when he looked for positivity in people.

It baffled his friends how he persuaded and inspired people on a journey of self-development. Almost everyone from his batch at the NDA has a story to cherish about him – Anuj, the human and the soldier in the making.

⁓

The National Defence Academy changed Anuj. When he went home on leave, it took Mani a while to accept the person he had become. The only change she looked forward to was of his marital status. The academy had changed her son for the better but she still wondered if he was at the right place. But the way he described his new life to his father removed all doubt from her mind.

For one, the academy had certainly made him more mature, resolute and assured of who he was and the role he was training for. His physical appearance, too, showed signs of the rigorous training. It was amply clear that he was making the best of his upbringing and the NDA's offerings. For an eighteen-year-old, he was a picture of uncommon confidence.

The young cadet was already gearing up for the next level of his training – at the Indian Military Academy. Not everyone who graduates from the NDA joins the IMA; some move on to the Air Force Academy or the Indian Naval Academy. After successfully completing three years at the NDA, cadets are sent to their respective academies for a year of training before being commissioned. Army cadets go to the Indian Military Academy at Dehrudun, Uttarakhand; air force cadets go to the Air Force Academy in Dundigal, Telangana; and naval cadets go to the Indian Naval Academy at Ezhimala, Kerala.

While at home, Anuj could not stop talking about his training. He would even survey domestic affairs like an inspector on duty.

He would walk around the house in a manner that often annoyed Karan. Prof. Nayyar, on the other hand, enjoyed this avatar.

Anuj spent a lot of time with his friends. He rarely went out without his motor bike. Girls would often approach him for rides but the answer was always a firm no. Lack of interest was cited as the reason for his refusal. Things changed during the vacation of February 1995, after he met Timmie in the playground of Army Public School where they both studied. He asked her out to the DSOI (Defence Services Officers' Institute) Club in Dhaula Kuan. And he invited her home and introduced her to Karan and Ashish. To see Anuj with a girl was nothing short of a miracle in the eyes of the sibling and the cousin. They giggled as they watched Anuj and Timmie engrossed in conversation in the drawing room.

The frequency of meetings and outings increased after that. The duo would take off on the bike, frequenting Priya and Chanakya cinema complexes, or loll at a park near Timmie's place. She would leave home on the pretext of going to college and studying in the library after class. On some occasions, Anuj would take Karan along to avoid suspicion and questions from his folks. Among other things, the couple discussed the future of their long-distance relationship. They promised to stay in touch through letters. Timmie had to give a friend's address for Anuj to send his letters. She did not want her parents to suspect anything before she herself could break the news to them. Anuj's parents got to know about them much before Timmie's family.

Distance makes the hearts grow fonder. Anuj's time away from home made him more considerate and appreciative of his family. This is what he expected of Karan as well. If Anuj found Karan arguing with Mani, he asked him to value her presence in their life. 'I live far off, so I know it,' he would say.

Karan remembers, 'There was this one instance when I spoke out of turn, in a tone louder than normal, with Mani about some school concern and he (Anuj) was really quick to notice it.

'In no time, he was all over me – not arguing, not scolding, but seeking a justification for my actions. His eyes were enough to make me realize that I had done wrong. He did not hit me, nor did he shout at me, he did not appear even remotely pissed off; though his activated posture, widened eyes and demanding facial features suggested otherwise. It's almost like, his body was scolding me and his mind was trying to reason with me.'

With his parents in the know, it became much easier for him to plan his days around Timmie. Poppin even cracked jokes and teased the duo in an effort to make the young lovers less self-conscious in their presence. He would often answer her calls on the landline pretending to be Anuj. But it was not always easy to trick the smart girl into mistaking the father for the son.

When Anuj felt that it was time to make his parents meet Timmie, the girl of his dreams, he invited her home one afternoon. It was a bold step for Timmie – to visit the family that she so wanted to be part of all by herself. There was a challenge in it as well as a bit of elation. Mani wanted to be sure that Anuj was serious about the girl. 'Just meet her once and I will ask you later,' he replied.

Mani rushed to the door when the bell rang that afternoon. Timmie was at the doorstep in a bright blue attire, confident and glowing. The next few hours were like a dream for the Nayyars. Timmie charmed them with her wit and good manners. The chemistry between Anuj and Timmie put every doubt to rest.

In the next few days, Timmie bonded with Prof. Nayyar over his love of music and photography, and with Mani over stories of Anuj. The mother regaled her with anecdotes from his childhood. Timmie returned the gesture by sharing titbits about Anuj as a boyfriend. The Nayyars' bond with Timmie grew with every phone call and visit, so much so that Mani and Poppin became Anuj's messenger one Valentine's Day. On Anuj's request, they fixed up a meeting with her at Vasant Kunj and handed her a bouquet of roses and a bag full of chocolates.

While Timmie bonded with his family, Anuj continued his training at the NDA. Mani's worries for him calmed – temporarily – every time she spoke to Timmie, but she knew that she could never have absolute peace of mind. It was a part and parcel of being the mother of a soldier. She even worried about his diet at the NDA, which was in stark contrast to what he liked to eat at home, which included meat dishes made by Poppin, loads of milk, *chhole bhature*, finger chips, pizza and more. But he had given in to a life of eating mess food. On vacation, Anuj forbade his mother from serving any of the dishes he would eat at the NDA mess. He would eat only what he liked, whether home-made or takeaway.

Anuj's father, on the other hand, was more focused on his development at the academy. Like any parent, he wanted the best for his child. But he was not after excellence alone. Poppin wanted Anuj to grow as a person and learn well. It is perhaps because of him that Anuj never obsessed about being top of the class or hankered for the post of cadet captain or a battalion cadet adjutant, which was somewhat the NDA equivalent of a head boy. His father emphasized on building a strong foundation for his IMA training and becoming an officer who could give back to his people, his squadron, battalion and nation. It is how Prof. Nayyar had inspired Anuj's true service to the country. For him, titles and gestures held no value without the respect of people.

Anuj picked up the characteristics of an officer of the armed forces quickly. He was heading towards a stronger physical build and was getting more proficient in military subjects. But there were still many miles to go before Anuj could be described as war-ready.

In the days following Camp Greenhorn, Anuj's NDA career took a different turn. He was now moving swiftly towards making a mark of his own. He made sure that his overall growth was good at the end of every term. He made sure that he acquired every trait required to become an army officer.

Anuj had set his gaze on some aspects of the NDA which he thought mattered more towards his development as a soldier. The Inter-Squadron Cross-Country Championship was among the targets he chose to pursue. He knew that the slowest runner of the squadron was as important to the final run as the fastest one. Thus, he set out to build and nurture a squadron that would be worthy of the coveted Glider Trophy, which is awarded to the champions.

The NDA and the army are complete fans of running exercises, more than any other athletic pursuit. Anuj, as Col. Thakur recalls, was unhappy with his performance on this count.

In the initial days, Anuj would complete a cross-country run in the fourth or fifth enclosure. These races are spread across various terrains, through jungles, concrete roads, hills and even creeks. There are bursts of continuous running followed by short breaks between flag posts to regain energy. It is between these flag posts that cadets switch positions, and as cadets fall behind or gain positions, ranks are given in terms of the heats in which the runner passes the finish line.

Anuj would practise at odd hours to improve his game. It seemed that he was convinced that a poor runner could not be a good army man. Even the stripes he had earned in other sports paled in comparison to his moderately good performance on the racing track. Anuj was the vice-captain of the volleyball team of the '90 Echelons. He was also one of the best in other track and field activities such as jumps (long, short and high).

'By the end of the fifth term, this chap used to clear most camp races in the second streak and some in the first enclosure as well,' says Col. Thakur. This remarkable degree of improvement was obviously the result of his hard work. Even the instructors praised Anuj's commitment to running. The hours of practice may have taken away from Anuj's study time but he did not mind.

Anuj's indomitable spirit had an impact on the team as well. The Echo Squadron still remembers his obstinacy towards winning volleyball tournaments. He would make the team train for longer hours because he was allergic to the idea of lagging behind or, worse, losing. He would even drag the players out for practice after dinner. 'Uncle (Prof. Nayyar) had given Anuj a night glow watch, which he would wear to our practice sessions at night,' says Col. Thakur. 'There were strict instructions for lights out after dinner but Anuj would not let the dark come in the way of his volleyball aspirations. We would curse him at times because he used the night glow watch to time us. We would end up thanking him, however, for pushing us to the hilt,' says the old friend.

Anuj developed a near-umbilical bond with the squadron. He was among a group of people who were equally driven and hard-working. None of them were out to prove anything or show off their skills. Their hectic schedule barely allowed time for anything other than training. And the focus of the training was on pragmatic learning, never on rote. Such factors contributed greatly in Anuj putting the academy on a pedestal. The honour of the iconic institution was sacrosanct to him. A word against it would invite his wrath. It would not be wrong to say that he bowed his head in respect every time he entered its gates. His respect for the IMA and the Indian Army was an extension of this very feeling.

Col. Thakur shares an anecdote to illustrate Anuj's sensitivity towards the image and reputation of '90 Echelons. On a Sunday – the one day cadets spent either lazing in their beds and feasting on goodies from home, or stepping out of campus for their weekly connect with civilian life – Anuj and his squad were engrossed in conversation over cold coffee. The brew was not bought from a store, but made in buckets on campus! Over mugs of cold coffee poured straight from the buckets, the cadets cracked jokes, chatted about a hundred topics under the sun and discussed plans for upcoming camps and terms. They were joined by cadets from other squadrons too and the afternoon seemed to be progressing well. Certainly, no one had expected tempers to run high over cold coffee.

The trigger was a comment from a member of another squadron, who seemed to think that the Echelons had much to learn in terms of winning a competition. Not enough passion, he said. He went on for about fifteen minutes before a splash of cold coffee shut him up. The coffee that dripped from his cheeks came from Anuj's mug. Flushed with anger, Anuj addressed the fellow cadet, 'The squadron is like a mother to us … And you can't ever say that your mother is better than mine, can you?'

This simple statement left a mark on everyone present there. No one had an answer or a quick comeback. He had drawn a line somewhere, and everyone seemed to respect the decision. Even the cadet who got drenched with coffee had newfound respect for Anuj after this incidence.

By the end of his sixth term at the NDA, Anuj was part of a dream squadron that could win any tournament they set their hearts upon. The squadron was not just for winning trophies. The members could put their life at stake for one another. In keeping with Anuj's craving for the Glider Trophy, the '90 Echelons put in their best to bring it home. It was a victory most special, something that the team had practised for over five terms, securing merit cards in sports events and acquiring mental skills in the process.

Between these routines of training and competitions and occasional light moments, Anuj graduated from the NDA on 1 June 1996. The graduation ceremony was an overwhelming experience for his parents, despite the fact that they reached late. A transportation delay in made them miss their son's graduation. Nonetheless, the Nayyars were happy to set foot on the NDA campus. It was like a pilgrimage to them.

Mani used her leave travel allowance to buy air tickets to Pune for the passing-out parade. When they reached the Delhi airport, they found out that the overbooked flight had no available seats. The professor borrowed money from a family member to book seats on the next flight. Karan even changed his shirt in the taxi that brought the family to the academy. By the time they reached, Anuj had already received his graduation certificate. But Anuj's initial disappointment did not last long. Mani laughed, 'After all, Anuj had graduated that day. A degree from the Jawaharlal Nehru University, a passing-out certificate from the NDA, in his full uniform … His sadness wore off soon.'

Later that evening, the young graduate took his mother and brother to the mess for dinner. Prof. Nayyar had to opt out because of the cap on the number of guests allowed in the mess. Anuj wanted Karan to get maximum exposure to the NDA from the visit. He managed to sneak him into the hostel that night and even shared a cigarette with him. It was the first cigarette between the brothers, and Anuj showed Karan the correct way to hold one. Anuj never encouraged his brother to smoke or drink but he would not have him do it the wrong way either.

As he waited for the family to return from the mess, Prof. Nayyar took a close look at the honours board of martyrs in Indian wars. It had the names of martyrs and recipients of gallantry awards from the wars of 1962, 1965 and 1971. When the others joined him after dinner, the father asked the son, '*Yaar,* Anuj, *iss mein ek bhi* Nayyar *nahin hain?*' (Anuj, is there not a single Nayyar on this list?)

Anuj gave him a knowing smile in reply. He seemed determined to be the first Nayyar on that board.

'He was on to something after his father mentioned it that day. Little did we know.'

After the NDA, Anuj joined the IMA as a gentleman cadet of the Naushera Company, Cariappa Battalion. This was another great opportunity for the officer in the making. The Tiger of Drass had just frisked the jungle and was now learning to hunt, lay the ambush and defend his land.

Gentleman Cadet Anuj Nayyar at the IMA: The 'Sher' of Naushera

'There's no denying that I see a perfect soldier in you. Go on with all our blessings.' These were the words with which Prof. Nayyar chose to encourage Anuj as he set out for the next chapter of his soldier life. Karan was mostly happy about being able to boast about his '*fauji*' (soldier) brother. So, after a short vacation, Anuj was off to Dehradun.

The cries of an ongoing drill greeted Anuj as he entered the campus of the Indian Military Academy. He walked straight to Chetwode Hall, stopped at the doorway of the prestigious building, nodded in acknowledgement of its legacy and entered it.

Anuj had set a target for himself – to become an officer by the age of twenty-one. He wanted to start early, so that he could spend decades in service and eventually gain prominence and maximum exposure. He wanted to lose no time in fulfilling what he saw as his duty towards his unit, comrades and country. His aspirations were aligned with the IMA credo: 'The safety, honour and welfare of your country come first, always and every time. The honour, welfare and comfort of the men you command come next. Your own ease, comfort and safety come last, always and every time.'

Anuj enrolled as a gentleman cadet in the Naushera Company of the Cariappa Battalion, which was popularly known as '*gaddha batallion*' as it was next to the banks of the river Tons. His batchmates say that his wavelength matched with most of the others in the company. It was a happy coincidence. Soldiers generally like to be remembered by their NDA days. They even end up using their NDA call signs as communication aliases in wartime. Those are the days when the youth learn from the company of enthusiastic compatriots; when duty makes an early impression on the intellect and moulds it for years to come. Luckily for Anuj, he found several NDA batchmates in the same IMA company. And he had the company of other like-minded gentlemen and some international embeds. The bonhomie worked wonders for the company. Each man gave his best, remembers Col. Chitrasen, Anuj's IMA batchmate. Anuj seemed to be the glue that kept everyone together. He did not just want the best for the company and everyone in it. He also wanted it to create a legacy for everyone to remember. Sure enough, his enthusiasm and motivation rubbed off on others. Soon high-ranking officers at the IMA started taking note of Naushera Company's above-average performance at the training.

The IMA training acted as a catalyst in Gentleman Cadet Anuj Nayyar's growth as a leader at the front. His organizational skills improved as did he physical prowess as a combat soldier. He was not guided by an aspiration for the Sword of Honour, which is awarded to the best performing trainee cadet. A place in one of the veterans and martial regiments is what he sought.

Amid the company war cry *'Sheron ke shera*, Naushera', these men found a leader in Anuj Nayyar. Naushera, a town in present-day Pakistan, was where the Sikh Khalsa army of Maharaja Ranjit Singh fought a fierce battle against Pashtun tribesmen in 1823. However, the war cry for the Naushera Company came from another battle of Naushera, which was fought in independent India. The hero of that 1948 battle was Second Lieutenant Rama Raghoba Rane, who was awarded the Param Vir Chakra for capturing the critical points of Poonch, Naushera, in Kashmir's Rajouri district, and Pir Panjal. Anuj shared the best of these two war ballads as he grew from a Punjabi Kshatriya to a second lieutenant in the IMA, before serving the nation with his life as a captain of the Indian Army barely two years later. The IMA batch of July 1996 brought together a bunch of NDA graduates, technical graduates and cadets from Sri Lanka. Together they formed a group called the 'Rogue Brothers'. Some members of the group could actually have gone rogue. But Anuj, who was always keen to support, guide and defend his mates, stood like a rock behind them. He gave each of them a sense of purpose, a reason to contribute towards the growth of the company. More than sparks of individual brilliance, he believed in collective good and achievements. This was in sync with the inclusivity of the Indian Army. It was also the essence of Anuj's nationalism, something that his father had taught him to cherish.

A soldier wears many caps. And Anuj wanted to do his best in every role, in combat and otherwise. He expected the same of his fellow cadets. He entreated them to be good fathers, instructors, orators and citizens. A soldier is a soldier even when he sleeps. And he is a beacon of hope to many. Anuj wanted to be an agent of change with his officer-like qualities. This could happen only if someone looked beyond the curriculum and picked up life lessons along the way. Nausheras to this date owe part of their success to Anuj who was always covering for the team and guiding them towards a glorious future. He transformed the Rogue Brothers into a symbol of excellence. And then he went on to become the Tiger of Drass.

As an institution, the IMA is so robust and royal that every cadet, be it ex-NDAs, technical graduates, foreign friendly cadets or combined defence services entrants, adopts its standards and forms a deep connection with their comrades and fellow mates. GC Anuj Nayyar was a worshipper of the squadron spirit. Just like the NDA days, he never remained quiet when anyone criticized, taunted or ridiculed his company.

Col. Chitrasen recalls a drill instructor from their initial days at the IMA. 'All our drill instructors were "ustad sahabs" to us. One such instructor tried to impress upon us the fact that the Nausheras' performance in recent years had been underwhelming,' he says. It was difficult to guess if his motive was to inspire the new batch of Nausheras or put them down.

While describing the grand passing-out parade, he asked the cadets: '*Tum mein se kisi ko pata hain ki* Naushera Company *pichhli baar* final tally *mein kis* rank *par thi?*' (Does any one know the position of the Naushera Company in the final tally last year?)

Col. Sarvinder, also a Naushera, immediately replied, 'Ustad sahab, first *aayi thi kya?*' (Did it come first?)

'No, my friend,' said the instructor.

'It must have stood second,' said another cadet hopefully.

Ustad sahab had the same answer.

This guessing game continued for a few more minutes. The Nausheras had counted till the sixth position but the coach's answer had not changed. He finally ended the suspense with the remark, '*Itni peechhe thi ki dhoondne se bhi nahin milegi.*' In other words, the performance was so poor that the Nausheras were almost invisible on the final tally.

Anuj, who was not paying much attention to the exchange until then, could not stomach this comment. That night he made his fellow Nausheras promise that they would work hard to restore the honour of the company, which was known to have given the army some of its best and decorated officers. It was a wake-up call for the gentleman cadets.

The camps at the IMA gave the young cadets many opportunities to prove their calibre. From treks to cross-country races, weapons training to guerrilla operations, their schedule was chock-a-block with activities that had their adrenaline pumping. These were also opportunities for Anuj to hone his leadership skills and motivate his company to a position of victory. He sought help and guidance from seniors and instructors along the way.

During one of those camps – Camp Torna – the Nausheras were asked to run through a circuit of eight to nine kilometres, trek uphill for another kilometre, complete weapons training after the trek and conclude with simulated drowning in water reservoirs. All of this had to be done while carrying weapons and weight packs of fifteen to twenty kilos.

'During these tests, it is common to lose one's endurance and fall, but the programme code does not allow the company to pass unless every man is accounted for. And thus, it becomes imperative for everyone to reach the enclosures and report at the end of each step,' explains Col. Chitrasen. 'Anuj and I maintained the company movement by keeping an eye on the group and helping anyone who was exhausted or had fallen along the way. At one point, we had three cadets who had to be carried along with their equipment and weight packs. And there's a reason why I say that these are the times that test a true soldier for his qualities as a company member, as a combat-worthy military man and a strategic mastermind.' They still had about 400 metres to complete the uphill trek, followed by the journey back to the base. Quite naturally, the group began to worry.

Anuj did not want to make it obvious that every man should choose between carrying their own load and worrying for their fellow cadets. He knew that before his mates came close to quitting, he had to be an example of motivation to them. He did not want his mates to make the choice between lifting their weights or of other tired mates'.

Anuj surveyed the bags lying on the track. He lifted each one and finally chose to carry the last bag, which was the heaviest of the lot. 'Others may now pick from the lighter ones and carry on,' he told the group. It was a way of telling everyone that they should come forward on their own instead of waiting for someone to go first, explains Col. Chitrasen. This gesture had the desired effect. Poked into action, the rest of the group immediately divided the work among themselves. And soon, the Nausheras were marching forward with team members and baggage in tow.

Anuj was a pillar of strength to all. He was touchy about failures. He viewed every failure – whether individual or collective – as his own. But he never let it get him down. He managed a fine balance between the serenity of a monk and the fierceness of a fighter. The outcome was what the world witnessed the day he conquered Drass.

He used to practice the same restraint at home. 'Why should others have the privilege of being any less daring, any less devoted than I am. Being inspired and being inspirational is necessary for one to survive,' he would say. Mani had once called Anuj to inform him that Karan was no longer allowed to drive his father's car. The fact that Karan was being barred from learning something was not so much of a concern for him as the reason. Karan had met with an accident and suffered serious injuries – the car was badly damaged too. Mani was worried about Karan getting hurt again, because he had not learnt a lesson in safe driving. Instead, his reckless driving incident became a fun anecdote to be shared with friends. She was worried that if unchecked, Karan would endanger himself and others.

Anuj asked his mother to allow Karan to resume driving immediately. He was not to stop until he had perfected the skill. Common sense would suggest that Anuj wanted his brother to win over the accident. But more than that, he did not want Karan to fear the vehicle just because he had suffered a few injuries. For him a strong mind was more important than physical endurance. He would say, 'Mani, an elephant also holds tremendous strength but the jungle bows to the tiger who uses his strength wisely.'

It is perhaps this conviction and resolve that made him the Tiger of Drass. He was not training at the defence and military academies to just become an officer of the Indian Army; he was preparing himself for the wars to come from the moment his father dropped him off at the station in Allahabad.

By the Company, Of the Company, For the Company

Anuj's time at the Indian Military Academy was devoted to the company. The day he heard about Nausheras' average performance in the recent past, he promised to salvage its reputation. He knew the hardships a person goes through in search of respect and honour. His father's life was an example of this. He had seen his father spend his entire life making ends meet, and he knew there was honour in it. He wanted to build on that legacy in his own manner. With this mindset, Gentleman Cadet Anuj Nayyar maintained a high regard for the schematics of competitive performance at the academy, at training courses and within his unit of the commissioned battalion.

During his third term at the IMA, Anuj took charge of putting together a team for an inter-company boxing tournament. To his dismay, he found out that the Nausheras did not have representation in all the weight categories. He looked for answers from the company appointments but found none. 'The appointments and others could have just said that they were trying, or their equipment was outdated, or that they lacked proper training, or a hundred other things; but the lack of an answer showed the missing intent of the company. Anuj decided to do something about it,' says Col. Sarvinder.

Anuj gathered some cadets and marched to the boxing ring for practice. He stepped into the ring and started punching the bag.

'After punching the bag for about ten minutes he stopped abruptly, sweating like hell, and told us, "I'm going to practise here every day until one of us can participate in each category ... Now, who's going to join me?" For a moment we couldn't fathom what he was saying,' says Col. Sarvinder.

Anuj was challenging other gentleman cadets to man up, almost taunting them for sleeping on their failures. Maybe they were dumbstruck by his audacity, maybe they did not muster up enough courage to accept the challenge, but no one stepped up to the task on the spot. Anuj went back to punching the bag, this time even more fiercely. After another ten minutes, he announced, 'Fine, have it your way then; I will sign up for all the weight categories and fight myself.'

That rattled everyone. He was unstoppable, despite a medical issue with his nose. 'I will see to it that there's a trophy for every weight category in the halls of Cariappa Battalion, in the name of Naushera Company.'

This declaration was enough to get his mates going. The boxing tournament that year saw Nausheras putting up one of their best shows. Even the fellows from foreign countries participated with enthusiasm. The result was exactly what Anuj wanted: a well-deserved silver medal for the company.

———

'Anuj had little interest in the regular course subjects as compared to the military subjects of strategy, platoon level tactics, military science, warfare, etc. We believed that these military subjects helped him clear the exams,' recalls Col. Thakur.

Anuj's education was not slave to rules, strictures and routines. He liked to keep room for departure from norm, a certain degree of spontaneity and even uncertainty. He did not have a formula for success. He was willing to take risks and face challenges.

Just like his aspiration of seeing the Nausheras excel in boxing, Anuj was keen on making the company count among the top teams at the Inter-Company Cross-Country Championship. Anuj had tasted success during his NDA days when '90 Echelons took home the prestigious Glider Trophy. He wanted a repeat of that success story. But the main obstacle in the plan was the lack of practice time. Anuj knew that the morning and evening sports hours were not enough to kick the Nausheras into motion.

'Curiously, he stumbled upon the idea of practising at noon,' said Col. Chitrasen. Anuj and his mates persuaded the non-commissioned officer (NCO) of the weapon armoury to allow them access to weapons and weight packs required to train.

The moment the team finished lunch, Anuj escorted them to the ground for extra sessions. Soon, other companies started complaining about the practice sessions. They thought it was special treatment. Anuj paid no attention to these voices.

The practice sessions continued till some of the weapons they used were damaged. Col. Thakur recalls, 'One or two weapons that we would borrow from the armoury lost the gas plug or some other part. Anuj was at the receiving end of the reprimands, but that didn't bother him.'

Like a good leader, Anuj took the blame for something that was not his fault alone. He also shelled out most of the compensation amount. He did not let the team's morale suffer because of the incident. According to Col. Chitrasen, Anuj did not want the company to be wary of trying something new or different. Despite the hiccup, Nausheras went ahead with the afternoon practice and ranked fourth in the tournament. This was a huge confidence boost for a company that used to be at the eleventh or twelfth position. Today the Naushera Company is able to maintain a decent standing in the annual ranks because of the winning streak that Anuj and his mates had started. Such was the influence of the team's leadership that they created a movement of motivation. The effects did not wear off with time; they evolved instead to find new aspects of greatness.

Anuj liked to play pranks. 'He was the kind of person who would fall sick if he didn't get his share of fun and mischief,' jokes Col. Sarvinder. In his 'fun' avatar, Anuj could target just about anyone. His batchmates, his best pals, his seniors and even his teachers.

One such target was a drill instructor who was new to the academy. The Naushera Company of 1997 was one of the first under Kaka Sahab Bhonsle's training. Both in terms of time and endurance, Bhonsle's classes were draining the group. They found themselves left with little energy or room for other activities. This was a problem for Anuj, who was more interested in cross-country races and boxing. So he and his course-mate Rohit Kaundinya decided to 'engage' the young instructor in a way that his sessions became less demanding.

Thus began the great 'Bhonsle operation'. His sessions became less about exercise and more about talking. Rohit and Anuj discussed everything under the sun with the instructor – from family to friends and battalions to battles. The conversations were occasionally punctuated with exercise. As expected, other instructors noticed the strange goings-on of Bhonsle's sessions with the Nausheras. They warned their colleague about being too lenient with the company. But that did not change Bhonsle's equation with the batch. He continued to shower his love on the Nausheras, thanks to Anuj who had convinced him that his colleagues were jealous of his popularity among the students.

It is not that Bhonsle was unaware of what his class was up to. It had become obvious that the Nausheras were having a bit of harmless fun at his expense. But he also knew that there was no malice or agenda behind using his class for relaxation. He even told the group, '*Tum log mere ko buddhu banaya,*' (You guys made a fool of me) but with a smile on his lips. Till date, many drill instructors remember the 1997 Nausheras fondly.

~~

Some people care only about results, some about the methods of achieving results. Anuj was among the soldiers who cared about both. Col. Thakur says, 'He would follow orders but deliver them on his own terms.' Anuj's twin targets of becoming an officer by the age of twenty-one and seeing Naushera climb the tally of inter-company ranking were within achievable distance during his final term at the IMA. Col. Sarvinder says that he motivated the batch to spend hours in the library as well, stressing the need for good grades in academics.

At the same time, Anuj refused to let go of any opportunity that would add to the company's list of feats. He persuaded Col. Chitrasen to participate in the annual cross-country championship despite a serious leg injury. 'I had come back from sick leave just days before the finals. I had injured my right foot in an accident and I could barely walk when I resumed classes,' he says. But his dear friend Anuj would not take no for an answer. He was sure that Col. Chitrasen's experience from the NDA days would help him finish the race and the team score well.

Col. Chitrasen gave in when he remembered how Anuj, with a bleeding nose, kept practising for the boxing tournament. His injury seemed too insignificant to even think of backing out. Powered by Anuj's confidence in his abilities, he managed to reach the finals of the event.

Even the cadets from Sri Lanka, who usually avoided contact sports, joined Anuj's boxing team because of his relentless persuasion. It turns out that Anuj trained them separately and they did pretty well. The Naushera Company secured the second position in the Inter-Company Boxing Championship.

Anuj had invited Karan to the finals. Despite the rules, Anuj managed to host his brother in the dorm. He offered Karan the bed and slept on the floor. He even gave him a tour of the mess and the drill square. Karan, however, was not the only guest to visit Anuj. He would sometimes find a reptile in the room, and other creepy-crawlies. But, a tired cadet can only think of sleep when in his room. Insects and reptiles were the least of Anuj's concerns.

On the night of the boxing finals, the company lit a bonfire to celebrate the win. When they ran out of firewood, the Nausheras used discarded furniture from the barracks to keep the fire going. This did not go down well with the officials. The Nausheras were punished. To make things worse, they faced questions about the boy in civilian clothes who featured prominently in the group photos. That boy, of course, was Karan. No one from the company uttered a word about him. This, too, irked the officials who punished the Nausheras once again.

Soon it was time to decide where to go after the academy. 'Anuj was interested in pursuing technical postings, in signals, engineering, etc. He had wished for better use of his technical insight and strategic excellence with a posting to the Signal Corps. He used to joke that it was about time that non-infantry units started recruiting more muscle.' In the months prior to the passing-out ceremony, every cadet has to fill out a form stating their choice of posting. They have to select between infantry and other Indian military sections. Anuj wanted to make an informed decision. In the end, his choices for infantry were in the following order: Grenadiers Regiment, Jat Regiment and Rajputana Rifles, all three known for high representation of martial clans.

Initially, Anuj had reasons for choosing technical over infantry. He wanted to stay within an accessible range for Prof. Nayyar and Mani. He also wished to put his understanding of strategic military subjects and signal/communication systems to good use. However, he took a turn by selecting infantry. His selection to the Jat Regiment came as a surprise. 'Maybe the officials found his profile more suited for an infantry role, which turned out to be true in the coming years,' says Col. Chitrasen.

On 7 June 1997, Gentleman Cadet Anuj Nayyar was commissioned in the Indian Army as a second lieutenant IC-57111W. He participated in the passing-out prade and crossed the

'Antim Pag', or the ceremonial last step, to take his oath of serving the nation, his fellow men and his unit.

At the end of the oath-taking ceremony, the newly inducted officers of the Indian Army threw their caps in the air. Anuj did not let go of his cap, though. He held it close to his heart as he walked over to meet his parents and his brother. The cap and the uniform seemed to be the shining armour of the gallant Nayyar.

That Anuj could have chosen another profession seemed like an impossible idea – the Tiger of Drass was already on the prowl. It was only a matter of time before he marked his territory. Meanwhile, somewhere in the offices of Pakistan military general headquarters in Rawalpindi, the first pitch meetings of the 1999 events were being laid down.

3

From a Cadet to an Officer

I am not irresponsible that I will die without fulfilling my duties for the country. I want posting in Siachen so that I can test my physical and mental endurance. I want to see how tough I really am.

— Capt. Anuj Nayyar, MVC

FOLLOWING HIS GRADUATION FROM the IMA, Anuj Nayyar joined the 17th Battalion of the Jat Regiment in August 1997. It was a momentous occasion for the young officer, who raised seventeen toasts during ragging to prove that he was not one to take any challenge lightly. He was among the fighters who guarded the regiment's honour with passion. It is said that when Maha Vir Chakra recipient Brigadier Desmond Hayde (3 Jat Battalion) was asked what makes a Jat fearsome in combat, he pointed to the company man next to him and said, 'The men fight because Major

Shekhawat fights. We fight because we hold nothing dearer than the respect we get back from our fellow men, family and community back at home. Our fear of losing that respect is what overcomes the fear of death.' Second Lieutenant Anuj Nayyar immortalized these values during his years of service.

The Jat Regiment has an illustrious history of over two hundred years. One of the most decorated regiments of the Indian Army, its success stories date back to the battles and wars it fought for British India, in Afghanistan, Burma, Africa and during the two world wars. Post-independence, the regiment led the 1948 combat against the Kabalis in Kashmir, against the Chinese army in the 1962 Sino–Indian War, against the Pakistani army in 1965, and during the 1971 Bangladesh Liberation War. This history made Anuj choose the regiment among his other infantry options at the IMA.

He had shown promise right from the beginning. 'It was a decent break, about three to four years, after which an officer trained at both NDA and IMA came to the battalion. I had confidence in him from the first day. I was second in command (2IC) of 17 Jat at the time and I knew Anuj was going to perform phenomenally as an officer,' recalls Brig. U.S. Bawa.

Anuj joined the battalion in Sri Ganganagar, Rajasthan, where he completed the initial unit training before he went for the 'Young Officers' course. Also known as the YOs, it is the first professional military training imparted to an officer of the Indian Army right after his commission. For an infantryman it is conducted at Mhow, a tinsel town near Indore, Madhya Pradesh. An officer after a year of exposure at unit-level leadership, training and tactics is exposed to military tactics at platoon and company level with an overview of activities at battalion level. It comprises weapons and tactical training, over a period of less than a year. The first professional military academic exposure, it is seen and attempted vigorously by the officers. The organization also takes a serious view of it in teaching and assessment with the aim to set the highest standards for the officer and the army. Officers individually undergo pre-course training at unit level to excel in the course. Generally, the same batch officers attend the course together. It sets a tone for a course social, without undermining the rules of competitiveness.

An officer is selected for the course as per the seniority of his merit. At a young age the seniority is primarily the passing-out merit of the academy. The other parameters of vacancy, officers' medical health, peace or field engagement, his preparedness and so on also come into play for the nomination. However, it is a mandatory course and all officers have to attend it sooner or later.

What is more significant is the motivation and diligence with which the officer completes the course. In pursuit of excellence is the norm. It also sets the tone and differentiates between good and better officers. The jawans that a young officer commands also judge him for his professionalism based on his performance in the YOs.

Anuj, knowing its importance, wanted to complete the course at the earliest. For him doing well on the YOs was a defining moment of transformation from an officer to a professional military leader. He prepared himself for the YOs training at Mhow. To excel was his mission and attaining the highest standards was the goal.

From day one, Anuj, true to his above-average interpersonal skills, chose to build a strong relationship with fellow officers and soldiers. Like all battalions of the Indian Army, 17 Jat required every officer's acclimatization with the unit. Every new officer stayed in the barracks, ate with the soldiers and carried out day-to-day unit proceedings under close supervision of the sepoys.

Brig. Bawa says, 'I still remember the joy Anuj expressed the moment I informed him about the officer–sepoy bonding exercise.' Anuj went ahead with it with great enthusiasm.

The ritual worked wonders for Anuj's reputation and image among seniors and classmates. Col. Ashok Thakur recalls Anuj as the go-to officer for the unit whenever anyone had a doubt. It was always better to run it by 'Anuj sir', they held. He was also the most flexible in matters of granting leave and permission for extracurricular activities.

Sepoys interact and work under all kinds of officers. Some are authoritative, some polite, some are strict while some are lenient. Anuj seemed to have struck the right balance of authority, friendliness and understanding, according to Brig. Bawa. It takes time for a unit to warm up to an officer. That they accepted Anuj wholeheartedly was proven by the number of times they invited him to dine with them in the barracks, long after the acclimatization exercise was over. There, under the shade of trees in summer afternoons or evenings, Anuj was seen breaking bread with the unit, sipping lassi from tall glasses and regaling them with childhood and training-day stories.

'Anuj didn't demand allegiance,' says Brig. Bawa. 'He believed that the sanctity of the unit came from each individual in it, and unless everyone was equally in sync with the common goal and acknowledged for their role, the unit would not survive.'

Brig. Anil Sharma, who became the second in command of the 17 Jat when Bawa, then a colonel, took over as commanding officer (CO), remembers Anuj as the officer he thought would become a high-ranking army official. 'He met every criterion of an ideal officer. Even seasoned officers would shy away on seeing such a driven youngster in the battalion. You would always find him training for something or the other,' he says.

At IMA and NDA, Anuj was more focused on becoming an officer. During his battalion days, all he wanted and worked towards was becoming a good officer. And it's not like he took time to sink into the routine or align with the working of the unit. He made his way through the general proceedings of the battalion and moved towards the next step to being a ranking army officer in no time. Brig. Sharma says, 'I had never seen such a driven officer. He would sign up for everything, volunteer for every official or unofficial activity that gave him all kinds of exposure.'

The competitive spirit in Anuj failed to rest even at the battalion level. He was the officer who was always preparing for some competition or the other. He infused the barracks with the same spirit, guiding them on volleyball and basketball courts, and also learning from them in exchange. The summer of 1998 saw a host of new players from the barracks, all thanks to 'Nayyar sahab'.

The Indian Army issued a collective memorandum to redefine the hierarchy of fresh IMA cadets and discontinued the position of second lieutenant. All second lieutenants were to be promoted to lieutenants, upon their CO's approval. Anuj could not contain his excitement when he heard the news. He called Delhi and informed his parents that they would soon be receiving a letter of promotion. And that's how Lieutenant Anuj Nayyar came to be. This development gave him the push to apply for the YOs. It was more about pushing the envelope than rising through the ranks.

While Anuj chased his goals at Sri Ganganagar, his girlfriend Timmie prepared the ground for marriage talks between the two Delhi families during the lieutenant's vacation. She kept Anuj in the loop as much as he shared his daily updates and plans with his father. The professor kept writing to the son and sending him gift parcels. His father was living his aspirations through the young officer and was not shy to show his admiration for him.

It was during a call that Anuj mentioned his Siachen dream to his father. 'I would like to serve at Siachen someday. I'm preparing for it … I would like to challenge the heights and see who is more resilient – me or the glacier,' he said. He had decided to submit a formal request to serve at Siachen upon his return from Kargil. Siachen indeed missed a chance of locking gaze with a warrior.

Anuj's application to the YOs was initially rejected. Everyone including Brigs. Sharma and Bawa were in denial. But destiny had a surprise for Anuj. Just when he was about to leave for Delhi on a short break, his application got accepted.

The 17 Jat Battalion had a tradition of pre-training officers for the Young Officers' course, so that every officer who attended it came out with good scores and ranks. Brig. Bawa did the same for Anuj. He recalls, 'Before we could ask him for it, Anuj himself promised to secure an alpha grading in the course. He attended every pre-training session with utmost interest.'

Anuj knew that his success was attached to the honour of the battalion and the trust of his seniors. For the first time in his career, he yearned for good grades and scores, and strived towards them. Col. Chitrasen, his NDA friend who became his roommate at the YOs institute, says, 'To us, it seemed like he was making amends for the ranks and grades that he had lost in NDA and IMA. He was making up for his academic might, now that he had proven his excellence in the non-academic curriculum. But we were wrong.'

From his IMA days to his time at the battalion, Anuj had matured beyond his years. It seemed the pips had transformed him. His views and standards were the same; his approach was new. He went to the YOs training with a deep regard for protocols. He wanted to see if he could afford to rank by the book. This was another challenge for him, an intellectual challenge. This was his real graduation from an IMA-graduate to an officer.

In February 1997, before joining the YOs, Anuj was diagnosed with jaundice at the military hospital. He was immediately admitted for a ten-day treatment and Timmie ensured that the young officer received special attention from the staff.

The confines of the hospital bed were like prison for an active man like Anuj. There, too, he managed to sneak away from the facility to visit Timmie. 'I will kill this jaundice with the spicy food that they keep me from having,' he would tell her. Bunking hospital became common for Anuj and the two of them spent time visiting their favourite spots in Delhi.

The extra time with Anuj helped Timmie make a decision. She did not want to wait any longer and informed her parents about their relationship. Timmie's family embraced her choice with open arms and agreed to their match. Anuj being from Echo Squadron worked some charm on Timmie's father. At their first meeting, Anuj and Timmie's father spent more time talking about the IMA and the NDA than Timmie or the marriage.

Timmie's parents visited the Nayyar residence soon after and both families made the best use of the extended holiday by finalizing the date of the engagement ceremony. The function was held at a farmhouse and the two families came together to celebrate. Even their horoscopes seemed to proclaim the duo's compatibility; Mani recalls that thirty-five out of thirty-six gunas (qualities) matched on their astrological charts.

The betrothed danced to various romantic songs on the night of their engagement. Anuj seemed to be free and at peace. Free because his love was no longer a secret, and at peace because it had won social and familial sanction. It's rare for a soldier to show emotions. But when he does it, it adds to his character.

During this break Anuj also spent time with his father discussing the upcoming training. Just two days into the stay, he shocked the professor by saying he did not want to ride the heavy Bullet any longer. 'Get me something faster and sleek this time,' he demanded of the man who had mortgaged his beloved cameras and wide-angle lenses to pay for the vehicle that his soldier son had gotten tired of. Anuj's intention was to take the bike to the training.

The Bullet was soon sold and a brand new RX100 procured for the young Nayyar.

The young lieutenant managed to sneak in the vehicle despite the rules and his new obedience to protocols. The bike became Anuj's ticket to freedom after class.

After the course, a string of events led Anuj to 7 July 1999, the day he left his indelible mark on the hills of Drass and in the heart of the nation.

~~~

The army's Young Officers' course is the first training course that every young officer undergoes after being commissioned. To everyone's surprise, Anuj's call for the course did not come through in the first list. Bawa, then second in command, was 100 per cent confident that a clerical error had to led to this. Anuj, despite the setback, continued with his pre-course training. Soon enough his application was accepted. He had to report at the Infantry School,

Army War College in Mhow, Madhya Pradesh for the eighty-fifth YOs.

Anuj's NDA training was all about gaining physical and mental strength to be a cadet. IMA taught him the 'spirit of the company'. YOs brought out the best in him as an officer. Col. Chitrasen says that Anuj never slogged for good grades. 'To him, doing things the right way and making progressive changes to norms was more aspirational,' he says.

At the Infantry School in Mhow, officer Nayyar was a more organized version of his NDA and IMA selves. He planned his day in advance and his schedule had the perfect balance between hours of study and relaxation.

YOs was also a fiesta as all the IMA and NDA colleagues got together after being commissioned and spent time with their respective units. Col. Sarvinder says, 'It's almost a pre-inclination, a kind of cognitive pull, which makes people find their way back to their NDA classmates at the YOs. Lieutenants search for their NDA fellows and share rooms with them. But with us, it was the Nausheras who shared rooms … The credit, of course, goes to Anuj. He was the key to our bonds.'

While the days at the YOs were meant for training and practice, the nights were for spending time with their mates. The Infantry School at the Army War College did not allow trainees to keep personal vehicles. Anuj was one of the few who managed to get his bike with him. Col. Chitrasen, his roommate, remembers the constant challenge of keeping the two-wheeler safe from the prying eyes of their seniors. 'We couldn't keep it within the college premises, couldn't leave it with the locals, but it seems Anuj was the concierge of all trades,' he says. Anuj and another IMA fellow Vishal Dubey parked their bikes next to a public call office (PCO). The PCO owner's allegiance to the two officers was due to the large volume of business that came from the long-distance calls they made to their families, girlfriends and friends.

One day, at the end of a week's intense training, officers Anuj, Sarvinder, Chitrasen and Vishal decided to take off to Indore and stay overnight before returning to Mhow. The gang of four used their two bikes for the trip. Anuj and Vishal rode the new RX100. Somewhere on Mhow Fort Road, near the crowded DSOI Circle, Sarvinder decided to overtake a vehicle – by trying to manoeuvre between two trucks. Pillion rider Chitrasen narrates, 'The space between the trucks was enough for only one person but Sarvinder managed to take the bike through it. But after we crossed the trucks, we emerged behind another vehicle that had stopped dead in its tracks. Our bike was now swinging in the air like a kite and Anuj was maintaining his course right behind us.' The group escaped a collision by a whisker but the incident rattled Chitrasen who, as Sarvinder recalls, hurled abuses at the latter and decided to ride pillion with Anuj.

Chitrasen probably thought that the worst part of the ride was over. Little did he know that another brush with danger was awaiting them just a few kilometres away. That near-accident, Chitrasen claims, is still fresh in his memory.

At the next crossroads, a massive truck, speeding at about ninety kilometres an hour, came in the way of the group. It turned 270 degrees without slowing down, making Sarvinder lose his balance. He fell of the bike along with Vishal, while Anuj was only a few metres behind. Only a miracle would have stopped Anuj's bike from ramming into his friends who were sprawled on the road. 'That moment, Anuj made an important decision,' says Chitrasen.

A decision that showed his selflessness and concern for others, the quality of putting himself second.

Anuj asked Chitrasen to jump off the bike so that he could lay down the vehicle in order to prevent the accident. Chitrasen obeyed, landing on his rear. His wallet inside the back pocket of his trousers cushioned him from injury. As he gathered his wits, he saw Anuj tilting the bike. 'He slid under the bike before he let go of it,' Chitrasen continues. 'His swift thinking saved lives that day.'

The officers decided to celebrate the escape over drinks that night. They drank until wee hours of the morning. 'It was the last time we were together before Anuj returned to his unit, which then left for Kashmir,' rues Chitrasen.

Anuj made good on his promise to Brig. Bawa and secured an alpha grade in the Young Officers' course. He went home for a few days to celebrate this feat with his family.

While Anuj was breaking sweat at the YOs, the Nayyars back home were busy with the arrangements for the officer and Timmie's wedding on 10 September 1999. Shopping for jewellery, garments, wedding clothes and accessories were in full swing when Anuj came home after the course. Mani recalls the day he tried on the groom's clothes. The father was busy finalizing a car that he wanted to gift the couple: a golden Zen. All that was left to complete the groom's look for the big day were the *jootis*, the ceremonial shoes.

Timmie was an enthusiastic participant in the shopping excursions. She remained glued to her fiancé who often told her 'till death us do part'.

Sadly, that is what happened.

Verities Maketh Warrior

Anuj Nayyar's last break was not spent in just shopping for the wedding. He took out time to visit relatives and friends. He even attended a dinner at Brig. Bawa's residence, his second in command and lieutenant colonel at the time, where he introduced Timmie to the host.

When he heard that his unit was being posted in the Kashmir Valley as Corps Reserve, he was ecstatic. He told his father, 'One step at a time, Dad! Siachen is closing in day by day. First the Kashmir Valley and then the Siachen Glacier.' That day he went out with Timmie and Karan, after which he started to prepare for his new posting.

The unit was posted in an area named Khrew, under the Pulwama district of Jammu and Kashmir. Anuj joined as Charlie Company 2IC. Corps Reserve, the Indian Army's reserve forces, are first responders in war-like situations. Different companies of the 17 Jat were posted in various pockets to carry out counter-insurgency raids, search operations, patrolling, deep surveillance of active areas and other activities.

A few other companies of the battalion were already posted in adjoining regions. By the time the 17 Jat companies reported, the battalion had already covered the Pir Panjal range and was surfacing at Bafliaz, a garrison town in the Poonch district. By the end of 1998, Charlie Company was conducting raids and search operations in Sonamarg and Tutmari Gali. These were the known hotspots of insurgency.

Anuj had been the commander of a Ghatak platoon – a reconnaissance unit – at Sri Ganganagar. He continued to hold that position in Khrew and subsequent operations. Ghatak platoons are

Indian equivalents of the Patrol Platoon of the British Army or the STA Platoon of US Marine Corps. Anuj, being physically fit with good credentials in strategic planning and leadership, was given this position despite not having attended the commonly preferred commando training course to lead a Ghatak platoon.

In Khrew, he participated in a counterinsurgency (CI) operation – 'Operation Aghao' – with Ghatak platoons of other Corps Reserve. It was a three-day operation that involved the search and rescue of local residents in order to capture fifteen to twenty suspected militants. But before these men could be tracked, some of them fled while a total of eleven militants were killed. The company's 2IC Officer Madan lauded Anuj for his first CI operation in the Valley. Weeks later when he was allowed to call his parents, Anuj told them about his performance in the operation. Mani, of course, worried about his safety but Anuj managed to reassure her through his letters.

Anuj continued his sports activities in Khrew. He encouraged everyone to take part, not just for motivation but also in preparation for sudden, unexpected challenges.

Ghatak competitions are national-level tournaments for Ghatak platoons. These are not sports events but include military operations, drills and joint exercises between Ghataks from different units. Among other things, these tournaments have weapons training, high-altitude guerrilla warfare training, interception attacks and open-field warfare exercises.

It was evident from the performance of the 17 Jat Ghatak Company in Sri Ganganagar and other national-level tournaments that there was no other contender for the winning spot. The commanding officers decided that 17 Jat would organize the events, not participate or contest. Lt Nayyar was entrusted with the task of planning and executing them.

It was during this Ghatak tournament that Anuj met Col. Paresh Gupta, then a lieutenant like him, once again. They had been classmates at the YOs. Gupta asked Anuj to help his team in the competition. Anuj knew his friends well enough to have an answer for such situations. He said, 'I won't handhold your men to the victory post ... because that would be demeaning and I know that that's not what you're asking for. I'll try to give them cues to help find their own way. They still have to understand and act on their own.'

Gupta responded, 'I'll take what I can for now.'

Despite Anuj's guidance, Gupta's team lost. Many senior officers lauded Anuj for leading the event. The operation included a twelve-hour trek up and down a certain hill, which Anuj aced along with every other participant. Heavy and relentless showers made it nearly impossible to complete the competition.

Naib Subedar Manoj Kumar from 17 Jat's Charlie Company says that Anuj chose to not abort the events. He argued that if participants were unable to overcome unexpected challenges during training, they may as well forget about doing so in real life.

Kumar adds this about his former commanding officer: 'He had this nature of pushing the limits for himself and inspiring the same in others. His approach might not have been by the book, but he taught us a lot more than what we would have learnt on the job. No soldier left behind and 100 per cent delivery – I can sum his guidance in these two points.'

After the success of the Ghatak competition, Anuj was asked to participate in high-command operations, which were carried out on the basis of intelligence on high-insurgency areas.

Brig. Sharma explains the operations: 'In those days, Corps Reserve would set up patrol points at all prime ingress points during fall and winter. These were the areas where militants and radicals would cross the border to be taken in by safe houses in the Valley. Each ingress point had to be monitored by one or two officers with five-six soldiers. Anuj was at a post near Rajouri area when we were informed that ten militants were trying to cross the Pir Panjals. Along with troops, Anuj, Deepak Rampal, Padam Janghu and I were assigned to take care of the matter.'

From their position, Anuj and his colleagues could spot the militants only after a trek uphill and down to the plains. 'It was a three-day trek,' continues Sharma, 'but Anuj announced that we'd do it in two days or less.' It was the month of January and the team was aware of the difficulties of completing the trek in the snow-covered terrain. Anuj, who was put in charge of several soldiers, did not stop even while negotiating snow that was five inches thick. When a team member who was short of breath found it difficult to continue, Anuj waited a good five to six hours before taking his LMG (light machine gun) rifle and leading on.

Brig. Sharma realized why it was important for Anuj to wait before stepping in and taking over. He did not want to rob the soldier of the chance to bounce back. He wanted his colleague to overcome the physical limitation with mental strength. When Anuj was satisfied that the man had done all he could and there was a genuine need of intervention, he neither took time nor permission. He just took the rifle, loaded himself up and continued. At the peak later that night when Sharma, then a lieutenant colonel, asked him about what happened back there, Anuj said: 'I needed to check if I had enough in me to take on some extra weight.'

'I knew he was lying,' says Brig. Sharma. 'I was both amused and proud that here was this leader whom I had mistaken as a mere lad. And then I asked him if he was tired from the trek.'

'Nah! It's routine stuff, sir. I think we could be back before schedule if we stretch a bit,' Anuj had replied.

Sharma believes that 'a magnetic pull towards the enemies of the state' worked behind Anuj's indomitable spirit and energy. 'He couldn't stop himself when he knew they were around. It's also disheartening that this enthusiasm might have led to his martyrdom. He would have made a great CO someday,' Sharma concludes with a sigh.

Given the nature of his experience and activities in the battalion, Anuj was due for a Ghatak course, also known as commando training course, at Junior Leaders' Wing, Infantry School, in Belgaum, Karnataka. Before leaving for it, Anuj was once again given a pre-course training by the Ghatak platoon commanders of the company.

Anuj was granted leave to gather his belongings for the course. But it was curtailed due to the insurgency in Kargil. All officers of the battalion were called in for postings at critical positions. At that time, the Kargil insurgency was merely a military wire doing the rounds within the high command.

For Anuj, this was both a moment of reflection and sadness. He was sad for the loss of a great opportunity. This was one course he did not want to miss. It was pivotal to his vision of becoming a true combat-proficient soldier. Mani says that he did not lose hope though. He was sure he would make it to the next batch and get better grades. And Poppin was proud to see his boy become a superior soldier with each passing day, both in body and spirit. He would say that he felt like he was running the tracks with Anuj.

Col. Deepak Rampal, who was Anuj's sparring partner in boxing at 17 Jat, had assured Anuj of a seat at the next commando course. For the time being, the young officer was raring to be in combat with the adversary.

Anuj joined the operations at Uplana Camp in the Baramulla area before moving towards the Chitrakoot post, where he was part of a CI operation of reinforcing multiple posts up the Valley. These were high-altitude posts at 13,000 feet which had to be rationed with supplies and recaptured in case of insurgency. All these operations were conducted while Corps Reserve received information of insurgency in Kargil and neighbouring regions.

It was May 1999 by this time and the air was rife with rumours of military tension at the borders. But most did not take it seriously until there was word from the high command. Around February that year, reported escalations around National Highway 1A were looping across internal channels while the Indian prime minister was on a peace trip to Pakistan aboard the Sada-e-Sarhad bus service plying between Delhi and Lahore. The commanding officer of 17 Jat had even held a durbar of the platoons and units who warned him of a war-like situation with high casualties estimated. Thankfully, nothing came of it after the two neighbours took steps to defuse the tension.

This time, too, the intel was the same, at least for the ground units, Corps Reserve and the units that were not the first responders.

As mules were loaded at the operating base for the journey to the posts, Anuj and his team members took some time off to stroll along the cliffs with CO Bawa. During their walk, they noticed a steady stream of Tatra trucks driving past them. Bawa knew that it meant something for him and the men under his command. He told Anuj that the same vehicles, loaded with mules and supplies, will be used to ferry his soldiers to Kargil. 'Be prepared,' he warned.

The Kargil insurgency was still viewed as a routine affair that was being handled by units closer to the scene. No one quite knew its magnitude. It soon emerged that the infiltrators had absolute tactical upper hand and the Indian Army was struggling with intelligence.

Anuj asked if everyone should start packing right away. 'We are prepared, whatever comes our way,' he said stoutly.

Anuj's readiness for the situation – a situation that was fraught with tension and the prospect of death and defeat – warmed Bawa's heart. Later that night, at supper, the unit was told that it had to march to the frontlines in the Drass sector.

By then, Capt. Saurabh Kalia and his men of 4 Jat had been taken prisoners of war while they were patrolling the heights of the Bajrang post. The men of 17 Jat were moving for second-tier deployment at the Padmasan and Radhesar posts. These were regular operations needed to secure infiltrated posts. Anuj was part of the operation that was guided by intel that infiltrators had captured some high-altitude posts. Little did they know what lay ahead.

Many stipulate that the fight over Kargil started with the signing of the Tashkent Declaration after the India–Pakistan War of 1965. Facing embargo on supplies from global allies, Pakistan settled for a peace agreement brokered by the Soviet Union. Pakistan had backed down then but not accepted defeat. The fate of Anuj and other war heroes of Kargil might as well have been decided that fateful day – 10 January 1966. For Pakistan, Kashmir was too valuable a crown jewel to be forsaken because of one defeat, or two.

Pakistan suffered heavy losses in the Bangladesh Liberation War of 1971 and was made to sign an 'instrument of surrender' on 16 December 1971 and later the Shimla Agreement in July 1972.

That is when the story of Kargil really started. The humiliation that followed Pakistan's surrender, as Musharraf himself stated, was the moment of agony which made him resent the idea of a ceasefire. That day the Line of Control was established, a military control line separating the Indian and Pakistani parts of Kashmir, which included the regions of Poonch, Uri, Baramulla, Kel, Drass and Kargil.

The posts that were captured during the Kargil and Drass escalations were ones that were left vacant in hostile weather conditions. That was the agreement signed in Tashkent, Shimla and again in Lahore. The agreed solution: soldiers on both sides would leave their high-altitude posts in the winter months. It was agreed that they would leave their posts stocked with ammunition and ration. The winter of 1999 saw the snow receding earlier than usual, making it easy for militants, said to be in collaboration with the Northern Light Infantry (NLI) of the Pakistan Army, to take over the posts.

On 13 May 1999, suspicious movements reported by scouts and civilians in Ladakh started to appear credible. The high command drew up an action plan. Recently commissioned Capt. Saurabh Kalia (then lieutenant) was leading the fourth patrol that was sent to scout the Bajrang post, at 14,000 feet approximately, in Kaksar, Kargil. The weather that year was sinister with respect to border security. Before they could reach the safety of the post, a barrage of bullets and grenades fell hard on the patrol party of six. With the limited supplies that a patrol party carries, which is basically personal pouch ammunition, just one communication set, MRE (Meal, Ready-to-Eat) ration and a few hand grenades, Kalia and his soldiers held off more than forty assailants for as long as they could.

They were finally surrounded and captured on Indian soil. Radio Pakistan Skardu announced the capture of the men who were reportedly taken to the Skardu base, located in the Gilgit–Baltistan region of Pakistan, of NLI or Special Service Group. Capt. Kalia's body was returned to India on 12 June 1999. Reports claimed that there were signs of torture and multiple injuries on the corpse. By then the Kargil war had started. News of patrol party ambushes, killings, mutilations and strikes across the Line of Control poured in every day. Undeniably, it seared the hearts of soldiers guarding the terrain. It was a cruel summer in every way.

On the night of 20 May 1999, 17 Jat received a seventy-two-hour notice to climb down from the Radhesar post and move towards Ghumri in the Kargil sector. Anuj and his team were asked to report at the Hoshiyar Singh Ground, the base camp for 17 Jat and 79 Brigade, and await further orders. Until that point, information on the ground situation was so misleading that it suggested the presence of only fifteen to twenty militants on Point 4875 and Point 5140 combined; a maximum of ten infiltrators at Jubar Top, around thirty more in the Batalik sector and a maximum of ten insurgents at the Tololing post. All of this was a grave miscalculation. The real numbers were shockingly high.

The Pimple Complex is a range of cliffs, 11,000–14,000 feet high, in the Mushkoh Valley of the Drass sector. While Tiger Hill and Tololing are parts of the Kargil sector, where the NH1A lies precariously close to the Pakistani lines of defence, the Pimple Complex had a direct line of view of the NH1A crossing via the Zoji La pass right up to Sonamarg. These were the points from where the enemy could deal the deadliest blow. Infiltration at Tiger Hill and Jubar Top would have severed the link between Leh and Srinagar. The Pimple Complex could have opened a window for the enemy to deal maximum damage and prevented Indian troops stationed in the area from receiving any help.

By holding Point 4875, the enemy had a strategic advantage that expanded their sight across the Pimple Complex and a south-west angle on the NH1A. The whole range leading to Point 4875 included the Pimple Complex (Pimple 1 and Pimple 2), Rocky Knob, Whaleback, The Saddle (from the north-eastern ridge line held later by 2 Nagas) and South Spur. The first patrol parties to Point 4875 had already declared it as a trek filled with the dangers of slippery snow and steep climbs. Therefore, another position, Point 4540, had to be cleared for setting up a fire base. It was also a height from where the Indian soldiers could train their eyes on the enemy at Point 4875 and the Pimple Complex.

Charlie Company and 17 Jat were asked to recapture the Pimple Complex and secure Point 4875 and Rocky Knob. While gradients went berserk in the ranges of the Pimple Complex, the number of casualties were expected to be higher than what the Corps Reserve, 79 Brigade and 17 Jat had seen.

In the third week of May 1999, Subedar Desham and CHM (Company Havildar Major) Ram Karab were sent ahead for reconnaissance with a patrol party each to Point 4540. This was followed by an assault on Point 4540 and Rocky Knob, and then the capture of Whaleback, Pimple 1 and Pimple 2 to finally ensure a victory on Point 4875.

It is said that if Anuj and his team, along with other companies of 17 Jat, had not cleared the Pimple Complex, victories at the other points would have fallen prey to counter-attacks. Some even say that Anuj did what battalions could not in successive attacks. He cleared multiple enemy bunkers during a one-night assault, which led to the victory in the Mushkoh Valley. Another theory suggests that Anuj's victory in the Pimple Complex complemented the victory that Capt. Vikram Batra (13 Jammu and Kashmir Rifles) achieved at Point 4875. The aerial distance between Pimple 2 and Point 4875 was merely 300–500 metres. Having cleared this peak, Anuj and his company saved numerous lives. It is destiny that two of the greatest warriors of their time (Capt. Anuj Nayyar and Capt. Vikram Batra) fought and sacrificed their lives on the same day for their motherland.

Anuj did not think that he was carrying a great burden when he was gearing up for the assault. He was focused on flushing out the enemy. He wanted to keep the honour of his unit because 'squad *se badhkar kuchh nahin*' (nothing's greater than the squadron). All that he had learnt and acquired in his life were ready to be put to test.

4

'Did He Die Fighting?'

*I have yet to face an opponent who can win from [sic] me. I
want posting in Kashmir because I want to kill them for killing
so many innocent Indians.*

— Capt. Anuj Nayyar, MVC

A s THEY CLIMBED DOWN from the Radhesar post, trucks full of
17 Jat soldiers and officers started moving towards Hoshiyar
Singh Ground in Matayen, a mountain range a little off Drass that
served as a base camp for 79 Brigade. The collective convoy had to
give up their position at Tutmari Gali and proceed to Matayen via
Sonamarg and Zoji La. The Hoshiyar Singh Ground was to be the
base camp for 17 Jat.

The 1999 Kargil base camp for the 79 Infantry Brigade was the place from where fragments of news and distorted messages were feeding varied opinions among soldiers behind the combat lines. The 79 Infantry Brigade had 17 Jat, 13 Jammu and Kashmir Rifles, 2 Naga and several other units under its command. Brig. Bawa asked his seniors for extra time to descend from the post that his soldiers had taken seven days to reach. But it was not easy. With the continuous loss of units at the Tololing post and Tiger Hill, the Indian Army needed soldiers to check the Pakistani cover from all sides. The *paltan* (a full-strength regimental unit) was asked to leave their ration and ammunition at the Radhesar post and replenish supplies at the base camp. Anuj and other officers coordinated the movement of the battalion under instructions from 2IC Lt Col. Anil Sharma.

Anuj chose to travel in a truck with the jawans despite the offer to accompany CO Col. Bawa, 2IC Lt Col. Sharma and other officers of the battalion in jeeps. He wanted to boost the morale of the jawans and check on them.

During the journey, Anuj wanted to take a look at the photos he kept in his wallet. One of them was Mani's. He took one long hard look at it. Afterwards, Anuj looked for another photograph that was very special to him. But it was missing. A visibly rattled Anuj asked his companions if they had seen him drop the photograph somewhere or if they were playing a prank on him by hiding it.

Subedar Vinod Kumar, who fought alongside Anuj in Kargil, recalls that his frantic search for the missing item had begun to unsettle the jawans in the truck. The commotion woke up Sepoy Vijay, who was Charlie Company's radio operator in Khrew. He immediately knew what had happened and asked Anuj to calm down. He had picked it up after Anuj had accidentally dropped it and kept it with him to play a prank on the officer. He pulled out his own wallet and handed Anuj a photograph of Timmie. A grateful Anuj immediately fell back in his seat and spent the rest of the journey gazing at the photograph.

At Matayen, 17 Jat were given maps for reconnaissance and also debriefed regarding the situation in Drass. 'We were then asked to reach the 79 Infantry Brigade base camp in the Mushkoh Valley. Anuj and other platoon commanders were instructed to set up tents for the night stay,' says Brig. Bawa.

According to Brig. Sharma, pitching and folding tents was child's play for men who had been the reserve forces for the last one year, constantly moving across the Kashmir Valley.

While Col. Bawa went ahead of the battalion for a joint reconnaissance of the Mushkoh Valley, Anuj and his fellow officers got some time to call home. Anuj spoke to Mani and wrote a letter to Timmie.

He assured Mani that he was not posted anywhere near the action and that all he had to do was sweep an area of 100 metres for land mines. But all this while the fight was headed his way. When Mani and Timmie discussed the call later, she joked that 'when he was young he used to find baubles from my purse all the time, so finding mines in a 100-metre area is not going to be a tough task for him'.

At that point, media reports on the Kargil conflict were patchy. 'We were among the first families in India to get first-hand reports from our soldier sons. Anuj, as usual, was more excited than worried,' says Mani. 'His father didn't let me find out that he was posted in the line of action. At the same time, he saw to it that I knew just enough to not worry about his safety,' she adds.

Karan remembers Anuj telling their father that the army had all the necessary information needed to flush out infiltrators. He also asked the Nayyars to refrain from discussing the conflict with outsiders. The army did not want civilians to panic, he stressed.

On the night of 21 May, the Hoshiyar Singh Ground was shelled in the worst possible manner. It seemed the enemy had waited for the Indian Army to set up camps before they launched the attack. Being in the Corps Reserve, Anuj's unit was accustomed to moving in and out of tough situations at high altitudes. Lt Col. Sharma, Maj. Deepak Rampal, Maj. Padam Janghu, Maj. Ritesh Sharma and Lt Anuj Nayyar were asked to get their companies in order and depart for the assigned location in Mushkoh. The last trucks of 17 Jat rolled out of the campsite as a barrage of shells rained down on them.

On 22 May, 17 Jat reported at the 79 Infantry Brigade base camp. Makeshift tents and protective perimeters were set up immediately and rounds of strategic meetings commenced.

Unlike corporate boardrooms, the decisions at these meetings were not centred on productivity or cost; they were about maximizing kill radius of mortar shells or minimizing the risk of open assault. The very foundation of the Indian Army's High-Altitude Warfare School in Gulmarg, Kashmir, where US Navals, Royal Marines and the Royal Navy (UK) undergo specialist training, were laid on these grounds.

The Pakistanis were banking on natural cover and abundant ordnance to win this war. They probably had not factored in the robustness and agility of the Indian Army in the mountainous terrain. The Indian camps saw the commanding officer and his second in command hold long meetings with company commanders, company second-in-commands. junior commissioned officers and their men. It was decided that the battle of Point 4875 had to be fought from two ends. Point 4875 would be a separate front while the entire Pimple Complex comprising Pimple 1, Pimple 2, Pimple 3, Whaleback, Rocky Knob and other cliffs would be another.

The unit was safely positioned at 79 Brigade base camp, when trucks of injured soldiers reached the spot. Many soldiers were dead while others in need of critical medical attention. Anuj and his jawans carried wounded soldiers on stretchers to the infirmary. Subedar Man Singh remembers seeing Anuj talk to the injured soldiers in order to ease their trauma. 'Anuj sahab told me that shell-shocked soldiers are not efficient sources of intel. "We need the ground report," he said, "but asking a traumatized soldier about the situation would only agonize him further",' says the subedar.

Anuj eventually got the information he was after. 'The information helped us mentally if not strategically,' recalls Subedar Man Singh. 'Most of has read about war in books and fought in simulations and exercises,' he continues, 'but Anuj sahab wanted us to know what to expect once we reached there.' The state of the soldiers and the number of casualties made Anuj think about the scale of the conflict. It was clear to him that things were not as simple as they were presented.

Almost 50,000 rounds of AK-47, self-loading rifles (SLR) and tonnes of mortar shells along with hand grenades were transported to the base camps before Anuj and his team set out for the Pimple Complex base camp. They reached the location on the evening of 23 May.

Col. Bawa had given the initial operational orders to his officers in a makeshift tent at Hoshiyar Singh Ground. The attendees were Lt Col. Sharma, second in command of the battalion; Maj. R.K. Singh, commander of the Alpha Company; Maj. D.S. Punia, commander of the Bravo Company; Maj. Padam Janghu, commander of the Charlie Company; Maj. Deepak Rampal, commander of the Delta Company; Maj. Ritesh Sharma, second in command of the Charlie Company; Lt Anuj Nayyar, platoon commander of the Charlie Company; and Captain Madan, battalion adjutant. The mission: the recapture of the Pimple Complex, a combination of cliffs ranging from 11,000–15,000 feet in height.

Col. Deepak Rampal remembers how Anuj put up a fight to lead the company for an attack on the Pimple Complex. 'He would cite the merits of companies in peacetime activities and seek a chance for his team. He argued that the youngsters would never get their due chance. I wanted to keep him safe until we got the hang of the situation, but he pressed on,' he says. While the battalion seniors appreciated Anuj's enthusiasm, they still decided to plan otherwise.

The Charlie Company was part of the leading platoon, not the leading company. Though Anuj appeared to have made peace with the arrangement, according to Col. Rampal, he still aspired to do more than being in a reserve company. He felt his company would not get a chance to be at the fighting lines if his fellow platoon commanders did their job well.

Anuj was platoon commander of Platoon 7, Charlie Company. His team was tasked with providing fire support and reserve capacity to the lead attacks on the Pimple Complex. But destiny had something else in store for Anuj and his team. To capture what they called Point 4875 and the Pimple Complex, it was necessary to gain control of other strategic locations such as Whaleback and Point 4540. These points were where enemies had laid their first line of defence for the main positions. Anuj was on patrolling duty when Maj. Punia's company mounted an attack on Point 4540. Subedar Harphool Singh, Company 2IC, Bravo Company, led the attack on point Rocky Knob, twenty degrees southeast down 3,000 feet to the Pimples.

On 28 May 1999, Bravo Company of 17 Jat led by Maj. Punia carried out the Indian Army's first attack on Point 4540. Except the early reconnaissance reports, no one knew what was in store at these heights. A day prior to the Bravo Company assault, the patrol platoons of Subedars Deshram and Bhana Ram made first contact with the enemy. Maj. Punia planned the assault on the weakest enemy posts. With the help of 81-mm mortar fire and artillery support, his men pushed the infiltrators back to Rocky Knob. No casualties were reported and a critical point was captured – the battle record of 17 Jat was off to a good start.

The next morning Col. Bawa instructed Maj. Punia to continue the attack towards Rocky Knob. Blitzkrieg was probably what he had in mind. Leading the charge, Subedar Harphool Singh started the climb before 0200 hours. At 0400 hours, when the attack party was about 150 metres from enemy position, a shower of HMG (heavy machine gun) and UMG (uber machine gun) bullets started raining down on them from seven to eight ends. The alarming strength of the firepower prevented Subedar Singh from moving an inch. The attack party still held on. They moved positions and tried disrupting the flow of fire from a few ends. Unfortunately, that was not enough to save Subedar Harphool Singh and five of his men. They became the first war casualties of 17 Jat. Maj. Punia had to take the tough call of falling back from their attack positions at Rocky Knob after a word with Col. Bawa.

It became clear that the radio chatter and reports were wrong. The men raining bullets and shells on the Indian Army were no mujahideens with ad hoc defence lines. They were Pakistani regulars who were trained and well-provisioned. And they had deliberate defence lines set up against expected military action. It was an attempt to occupy and the preparedness of the posts was suited to this cause. The only way to sabotage their defence was through detailed planning.

The news of Subedar Harphool Singh's death made Anuj furious. He knew that Singh had been trying to find the right medical facilities for his critically ill child. He had finally heard back from a well-respected hospital. When he was recalled to active duty he thought that he could always return to his son but his country and his comrades required his immediate attention. Though the father could not go home, Anuj wanted to make sure his body reached his family. He volunteered to lead the team that would retrieve the bodies of the slain soldiers. Col. Bawa allowed Anuj and a small unit of Alpha and Charlie soldiers to go ahead.

The recovery team did not have it easy. Subedar Vinod Kumar of Charlie Company says the men faced heavy firing as they tried to retrieve the dead. 'As per the Geneva Convention, we had hoisted a white ceasefire flag to make it clear that we were there to carry our martyrs back home. But the inhuman people started shooting at us. Bullets flew past our ears as Anuj sahab and other team members tried to reach the fallen heroes,' he says.

The team managed to bring some of the soldiers back to the base but not the remains of Subedar Harphool Singh. Anuj was unwilling to give up the mission. Bawa had to intervene to convince Anuj and his team to suspend the recovery for the time being. 'I promised them that we'll take revenge for this inhumanity. I told

Anuj that the revenge for this peak would come from capturing the Pimple Complex and Point 4875. That was how he made peace with the situation,' says Brig. Bawa.

Through a series of discussions between the 79 Infantry Brigade commander, Col. Bawa and key battalion officers, it was decided that the battalion should conduct deep reconnaissance operations while setting up camps on neighbouring peaks. This would help them to understand the situation before mounting the next assault. They were given a month's time between 26 May and 1 July to set up ammunition silos and a firebase, and acquire detailed information of enemy locations. The units of 13 Jammu and Kashmir Rifles and 17 Jat were to carry out these operations within their assigned perimeters. It was also planned that by 5 July, in the first phase of the attack, the Alpha Company of 17 Jat would have established control over Pimple 1, while the Delta Company would be in control of Whaleback by 0500 hours.

In the last few hours of 29 May, Col. Bawa gave Anuj a surprise. He instructed the young officer and his Charlie Company team to survey the cliffs of the Pimple Complex, with support from the Delta Company. Their job was to climb the southwest and northwest ends of Pimple 2 to confirm enemy positions. Delta Company Lt Shamsher Singh and Charlie Company Lt Anuj Nayyar along with Maj. Janghu were assigned to carry out this operation.

In Brig. Bawa's words, he asked Anuj to go and meet the enemy and 'find out the place from where we would decide their fate'. He says, 'I told him to go deep into their hearts and minds so that no other Indian soldier dies for their cowardly attacks from hidden positions.' He knew Anuj was the right person for the job given his training and experience of conducting counterinsurgency operations in Khrew. But he did not know that Anuj would not just do a survey of the enemy positions. He would also leave his mark on the terrain. 'We were more confident about our strategies than the strength of the enemy. So there was no need to deploy Anuj at the front, but this recce changed everything,' the officer adds.

The recce put the number of soldiers and militants in the Pimple Complex and Point 4875 at seventy to eighty. These posts were well provisioned with medium machine guns, grenade launchers, 51-mm mortar and 120-mm mortar cache among other handheld weapons. Anuj picked his favourite spots to make his stand against the enemy; in the process, suitable positions for firebase operations for both phases of the attack on the Pimple Complex were also mapped.

The excellent job at a stealthy reconnaissance and accurate mapping done by Lt Anuj and Maj. Janghu helped Col. Bawa make his calculations. 'I concluded that this mountain complex would require not one but three battalions for low casualty and speedy victory,' he says. Brig. Anil Sharma acknowledges their contribution: 'They did such a great job that the angles at which our firebases were set dealt blows right at the enemy's head.' He added that the battalion had to report to the brigade command for suggestions after calculations indicated a high expense rate of ammunition.

Brig. Bawa asked the 79 Infantry Brigade Command to provide the requisite support for attacking the feature. 'I suggested that this task might require three battalions to mount a full-scale attack, given the reinforcement ability and the tactical advantage of the enemy. I was strictly against using artillery support, as were Sharma, Deepak, Punia and Anuj, and had faith in my infantry units,' he explains.

This was also when a ferocious counter-attack was being executed at 15,340 feet. The 18 Grenadiers led by Maj. Adhikari were putting up a fight to cover the first bases of the Tololing range. And Operation Safed Sagar had seen Indian Air Force fighter planes destroy posts close to Muntho Dhalo and Point 4388 of the Drass sector. At the same time, there were reports of escalated ingress from the Batalik sector into Chorbatla and Turtuk. Anuj and his troops got these updates from 2IC Lt Col. Sharma.

Given the nature of operations being mounted in Tololing and Batalik, the 79 Infantry Brigade Command inferred that the task of clearing Drass might take longer than expected. In the spirit of making calculated and bold decisions towards the greater good, it was decided that the battle of Drass shall commence after the battle of Tololing. The units of 17 Jat and 13 Jammu and Kashmir Rifles were asked to strengthen their positions while they awaited instructions for attacks on the Pimple Complex and Point 4875. In response to the opponent's deliberate defence strategy – the defence organized before contact is made with the enemy – the Indian side chose a more patient approach. The units were asked to utilize their time as an extended acclimatization exercise that would give them a chance to set up firebases in the hills.

Based on the intel gathered by Lt Anuj and Lt Shamsher, the spots for setting up ammunition dumps were finalized. Anuj observed the goings-on with great interest and patience and delivered on every task he was assigned. It was a miracle that he managed to keep his calm for so long. The conflict in Kargil was in a league of its own in terms of the challenges. The devious enemy was positioned in untraceable holes, with an unforgiving geographical disadvantage. It would break anyone, but not Anuj. In a letter to his father from those days, he wrote, 'I'm not that irresponsible to come home without a fight. I am not that person who would come back without winning this war, it's not what you've taught me.'

Thus began the long wait for the victories at Tiger Hill and Tololing. Lt Anuj would visit Col. Bawa daily and seek the latest updates on the Tololing battle. 'He was seated next to me when I got news of Lt Col. Vishwanathan falling to the enemy attacks,' recalls the retired brigadier. From 28 May to 28 June, the soldiers of 17 Jat moved heavy ordnance to the secured firebase in the Pimple Complex. They utilized the month for advance reconnaissance and ammunition dumping.

It is arguably this period that led to the swift victory of the Pimple Complex and, by extension, the Drass sector.

Each soldier in the leading and reserve companies had to visit the firebase before the actual attack. They were to get a good look at their holding points. 'Simultaneously,' says Subedar Man Singh, 'everyone was told to carry rounds of ammunitions and equipment so that we could set up our bases way before the command order.'

Anuj went on multiple reconnaissance operations during that month. His operations were pivotal in identifying the positions that gave the Indian Army maximum tactical advantage in the attack. Anuj applied every aspect of his training and education – from his schooldays to his time in Khrew – to the survey and supply operations. 'I had noticed his growth from a serious officer to a keen strategist in those few days. His eyes would search for details in everything. His sight extended beyond the range of our telescopic cameras. He was getting faster and faster in climbing to the post,' Col. Rampal says. He adds that he tried to replicate Anuj's mental and physical strength towards the combined objective.

Meanwhile, the shelling at Tiger Hill by the artillery units of the Pakistani Army had started affecting traffic on the roads to Ghumri and Zoji La from Sonamarg. These formed the main ends of the National Highway 1A that connected them with the Jammu base camps of the Indian Army. Ration supplies took a hit because of the disruption. Provisions would not reach the soldiers for days at a stretch. The men of 17 Jat learnt to deal with the situation with humour. While carrying cans of ammunition, they would joke, 'At least there's unlimited ammunition. We can live with food shortage but the enemy should not go hungry.'

The soldiers banked on ready-to-eat meals to survive the shortage of food. Fresh supplies would mean puri, sabzi and dried fruits for meals. Subedar Vinod Kumar says he would dispose of the old stock every time new supplies reached the camps. 'There was a big rock below our campsite where I would discard the stale food,' he recalls.

In the third week of their patrolling operation, 17 Jat units were close to exhausting their ration barring milk, sugar, tea, coffee and biscuits. Anuj shared his meals with everyone. He would only have the milk and carry on with his work. The supply scene looked uncertain because of the heavy shelling in retaliation to the escalation by the Indian forces in Tiger Hill and Tololing.

One day, Capt. Anuj asked Subedar Kumar if he could spare something to eat. 'He said he was hungry. I declined and shook the almost empty can of milk to show what I had.'

It dawned on him later that the rotis he had thrown away could be consumed. 'I told Anuj sir I would get him something to eat, but only after dark,' Subedar Kumar says. He kept his word. He went down the cliff and found the rotis. Back at the camp, Anuj, the subedar and another platoon solider lit the stove, crushed the hardened rotis and mixed them with sugar and milk to make about seven or eight laddoos. The trio ate the laddoos with relish, happy to have come up with a solution to the hunger problem.

Another time, Anuj and his team stood outside the ammunition NCO, waiting for supplies to carry uphill. Feeling impatient, Anuj complained about waiting too long when Maj. Janghu asked, '*Aur*

Anuj, *aaj kya le kar jaa rahe ho?*' (So Anuj, what are you carrying today to the top?)

Maj. Ritesh Sharma quipped, 'Anuj *toh sahab hai jawano ka*; *yeh toh* missile *le kar jayega.*' (Anuj is an officer of the jawans, he will carry a missile.) Sure enough, Anuj carried a missile launcher unit and a round of ammunition to the top that day.

'Anuj was where he wanted to be. He was living the war and readying himself with every passing day. I reckon had we been delayed any further, he would have gained the strength and rigour to take on the whole Pimple Complex and the Drass sector on his own,' says his commanding officer, Umesh Bawa.

In the next few days, the unit awarded wartime promotions to boost the morale of the troops and appreciate the work of officers. Col. Bawa promoted every havildar to naib subedar and every naib subedar to subedar. He said that for him every one of them was an officer and they could start considering themselves as one. That he would require from them the same training, the same performance and the same valour as an officer of the Indian Army. Second in command Lt Col. Sharma handed promotions to lieutenants and captains. One of the officers drew his attention to Anuj. The decision to promote him was taken in a split second. 'Well, hurry up and get me the pips then!' said Lt Col. Sharma to the officer.

And that is how Lieutenant Anuj Nayyar became Captain Anuj Nayyar on 23 June 1999, in the presence of Col. U.S. Bawa, Lt Col. Anil Sharma, Maj. Madan, Maj. D.S. Punia, Maj. Ritesh Sharma, Maj. Padam Janghu, and a few other mates. The young officer immediately wanted to inform his parents over the phone but the limitations of wartime communications did not allow it.

Anuj now had a bigger responsibility to shoulder. He was a leading platoon commander and a captain as well. He promised his seniors that he would not let them down. He had only one aim: recapturing the Pimple Complex. He turned to Lt Col. Sharma and asked, 'Sir, 7 July is your birthday?' The second in command was amused to find him talking about birthdays in the middle of a war. He nodded in reply. Anuj then pointed at Pimple 2 in the distance and said, 'That feature you see, sir? It's going to be my present for you this year.'

True to his words, Anuj secured the feature he wanted to gift him. 'I lost a good soldier. But I also lost a friend and a son-like figure the day Anuj died. We suffered many losses that day, but I was deeply aggrieved by his death,' says Lt Col. Sharma. Since then, he has stopped celebrating his birthday.

Anuj did more than just win a battle in Kargil. He left his mark on the lives of many through his compassion, humanity, team spirit and sense of humour. He embodied the best that a soldier can be. Anuj was the Jat battalion and every Jat was him.

The victory at the Pimple Complex was his gift to the nation. Like Abhimanyu, a brave and tragic war hero in the Mahabharata, Anuj led his unit through a labyrinth of bunkers to achieve success in the battle.

'Three Down, One to Go'

Tololing was won back, so was Tiger Hill. The stories of Lt Col. Vishwanathan, Maj. Rajesh Adhikari, Capt. Manoj Kumar Pandey, Grenadier Yogendra Singh Yadav were now ringing across the Kashmir Valley and the hearts of raging soldiers. On 3 July, Col. Bawa received orders to mount their attack. Both Tiger Hill and Jubar Top had been reclaimed that day. Tiger Hill had the tactical advantage of crushing any attack from the Indian side on the Pimple Complex. It was, therefore, necessary to get there before the assault on the Pimples.

The attack strategy for 17 Jat was already in place. The attack would be executed in two phases, and Anuj's team had pivotal roles to play in each. In the first phase, the Delta Company led by Maj. Rampal and Lt Shamsher Singh would mount an attack on Whaleback, which was the first enemy post en route the Pimple Complex. A simultaneous attack by the Alpha Company, under the leadership of Maj. R.K. Singh and Capt. Venugopal, would target the Pimple 1 peak.

In an earlier incident, while returning fire to the Pakistani troops somewhere between the Pimple Complex firebase and Pimple 1, Maj. Janghu was hit by a mortar shell splinter. This forced his transfer to the base medical facility. While Anuj was second in command of the Charlie Company, Maj. Ritesh Sharma was put in charge of leading the Charlie men as reserve force. Anuj and his men backed Maj. Rampal, while Maj. R.K. Singh took on Pimple 1.

As per plan, Pimple 1 and Whaleback were taken by both leading companies in the early hours of 5 July. Maj. R.K. Singh had initiated the dual attack on the night of 3 July. Before the enemy could hit back, Maj. Singh and his men neutralized two infiltrators and recaptured Pimple 1 under the cover of the night. The following night, at around 2100 hours, Col. Bawa received a situation report that Thumb Cliff had been captured. The Alpha Company kept moving through the night to reach Pimple 1. By 0200 hours the next morning, Maj. Singh and his men were at Pimple 1.

Capt. Venugopal and Subedar Om Prakash took separate attack platoons to bottleneck the enemy escape and attacked from either side of Pimple 1. By 0500 hours on 5 July, Maj. R.K. Singh had secured his position at Pimple 1 and eliminated most of the infiltrators. Some of them were able to manage a quick slip as they fled back to Pimple 2. The stealth and thorough elimination of enemy posts on Pimple 1 and Whaleback allowed the battalion to employ an element of surprise for the attack on Pimple 2. It was not until Pimple 2 was directly attacked that the enemy realized Pimple 1 had been taken. The Alpha Company went on record to establish that the firebase set up by the Charlie Company, led by Maj. Janghu and Capt. Anuj Nayyar, had proved a valuable asset in the Pimple 1 assault. Their accuracy in calibrating the mortar shelling posts at the firebase helped to deliver crucial hits as the Alpha Company led the attack.

Maj. Rampal had it a bit rough on Whaleback. By the morning of 5 July, the men of Delta and Alpha companies had taken their respective posts for the counter-attacks. The first wave of counter-attacks on Whaleback led to a considerable loss of ammunition for Maj. Rampal. His team was also crippled by the injuries of seven soldiers. Whaleback was won after a great firefight and it took more time than the stealth attack of Pimple 1. Because it was open from all sides, Whaleback suffered counter-attacks in the morning. 'Maj. Rampal kept sending me emergency messages, requesting more ammunition,' says Brig. Bawa. 'Anuj was there by my side when I got those messages, and I could see him getting uncomfortable with the delay in sending reinforcements.' Anuj and Maj. Rampal were like brothers in the battalion. So it was natural for him to feel anxious about the safety of the man he looked up to.

Anuj was packing his bags for the attack even before he was asked. After reporting to the brigade command and high command, Brig. Bawa walked towards the arms sentry to find Anuj readying his 'Pack 08' (a full-service marching order, or FSMO) for battle load.

Brig. Bawa continues, 'There was a common INSAS-SLR (main weapon), a 9-mm automatic standard issued pistol (secondary weapon), MRE ration and some magazines for both sidearm and main rifle. But then I saw something else – Anuj started to clean GP-25 UBGLs (under barrel grenade launcher) and kept one on top of his bag. He then started counting the standard 36-mm hand grenades. He somehow knew that it was time to start preparing. I must have stood watching him for a while before he realized that I was there. He just looked at me and said, "*Aaya* sir, *bas thoda sa aur*," (I'll be right there, sir, just a little bit more) pointing at the remaining grenades and bullet cans.'

At the same time, another bag was being prepared in New Delhi. Mani was packing sweets, woollen clothes, music CDs and a sacred thread for her soldier son. 'Anuj being Anuj tried to keep the severity of the situation from the family. In his last letter to his father, Anuj sympathized with Prof. Nayyar by saying, "I know you must be getting solid kicks from Mani for letting me join the army." It was from Maj. Ritesh Sharma that we got to know about his exact position in Kargil,' she says. Maj. Sharma, who was in Delhi before he was called back to Kargil for the Pimple Complex attack, asked if the Nayyars would like to send anything for their son. That was the last time Mani packed a bag for her son Anuj.

Timmie loaded chocolates in the goody bag at the Nayyar residence, while Anuj loaded his backpack at the camp with more bullets. The last time Timmie and Anuj got on a call was on 2 July. Anuj told her that an important mission might be underway and he may get another chance to perform well. He ended the call by asking Timmie to think of honeymoon destinations. It seemed Anuj was also gearing up for marriage but only after sending the insurgents to their right place – 'not back to their holes but straight to hell'.

KID ANUJ
Anuj, aged three, 1978.

FIRST BIRTHDAY
Anuj's first birthday, with his parents, 28 August 1976.

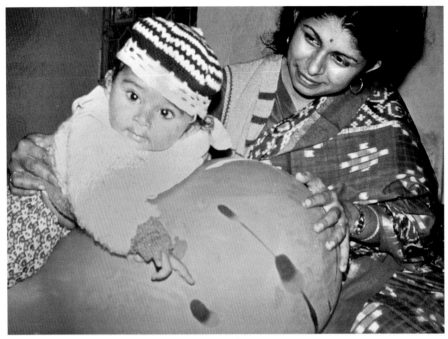

WITH MANI
Baby Anuj with his mother, whom he called 'Mani', 1976.

LIKE MOTHER, LIKE SON
Anuj with Mani, 1978.

THE TRIO
Prof. S.K. Nayyar, Poppin to his boys Anuj and Karan, at a family picnic, August 1980.

BIG BROTHER ANUJ
From left to right: Karan and Anuj with cousins Abhishek and Ashish, 1983. Anuj always looked out for his brothers and got them out of trouble many times.

BROTHERS
Growing up, Anuj and Karan were inseparable, 1984. The younger Nayyar looked up to his disciplinarian officer brother.

ANUJ WITH HIS FIRST GUN
Gunfights started early in child, and lasted his entire lifetime. Anuj with his cousin, Ashish, c. 1985.

ARMY PUBLIC SCHOOL
New Delhi.

CLASS................ SESSION 1984—1985 SEC..................

CLASS PHOTOGRAPH

The class fourth of Army Public School, Dhaula Kuan, 1985. Young Anuj can be seen standing behind the teachers (fifth from right).

NEIGHBOURHOOD GANG
Anuj with his friends from the neighbourhood at the tournament his father Prof. S.K. Nayyar conducted for them, 1987.

YOUNG ANUJ
In October 1990.

SCHOOL DAYS
Anuj with classmates at Army Public School, Dhaula Kuan, 1992.

MEN AT ARMS
Cadet Anuj Nayyar at the National Defence Academy's, Greenhorn September 1993.

DOWN IN THE TRENCHES
Cadet Anuj Nayyar digging trenches with his mates at Camp Greenhorn, September 1993.

Cadet Anuj Nayyar in NDA, 1995.

Cadet Anuj Nayyar in winter mufti at NDA, November 1995.

Cadet Anuj Nayyar in the Blue Patrol uniform at NDA, December 1995.

Cadet Anuj Nayyar in Drill Order uniform at NDA, February 1996.

NDA POP
Mani shaking hands with Gentleman Cadet Anuj Nayyar at the
National Defence Academy's passing-out parade, 1 June 1996.

POPPIN AT THE IMA
Prof. S.K. Nayyar visited his son during his training days at the Indian Military Academy. He poses for a picture with Anuj and his batchmate Ashok Kumar Thakur (left).

PUSHING THE LIMITS
Anuj at a cross-country run with his batch mates at the National Defence Academy, June 1996.

WARRIOR IN THE MAKING
Cadet Anuj Nayyar, in 'dhawa' position, a combat posture used to engage enemy in close combat with a rifle bayonet, at the Indian Military Academy, November 1996.

'90 ECHELONSS

The '90 Echelons of the NDA's Echo Squadron, batch of 1996. Cadet Anuj Nayyar can be seen sitting in the first row, second from left, 1 June 1996.

Anuj Nayyar in 1997.

Gentleman Cadet Anuj Nayyar in 6 Bravo
Dress (ceremonial) at IMA, February 1997.

A SMILING OFFICER
Anuj at his passing-out parade,
7 June 1997.

IMA POP

The Indian Military Academy's passing out-parade was a proud moment for the Nayyar family. Prof. S. K. Nayyar, Mrs Meena Nayyar, and Karan with Second Lieutenant Anuj Nayyar, 7 June 1997.

PINNING STARS ON HER STAR

Mrs Nayyar with newly the commissioned Second Lieutenant Anuj Nayyar at the Indian Military Academy's passing-out parade, June 1997.

FIRST POSTING
Officer Anuj Nayyar greets the commanding officer of 17 Jat at his first posting in Ganganagar, 1997.

TIGER IN CAMO
Anuj Nayyar, in the army's camouflage uniform of the Indian Army, 1998.

I AM PROUD OF YOU MY SON.
2nd Lt A. NAYYAR 17-JAT. 7/8 JUN 97.

WELCOME TO ARMS: The joyous commissioned officers of the IMA, Dehra Dun, after the passing-out parade. — HT photo by Pradeep Bhatia

THIS IS A PROUD MOMENT OF MY LIFE. ON THIS DAY THE
7th OF JUN 97 MY SON ANUJ NAYYAR WALKS IN THE IMA
GROUND. STANDS SMILINGLY IN FRONT OF HIS EQUALLY PROUD
& BEAMING MOTHER, WITNESSED BY HIS FATHER, BROTHER
KARAN NAYYAR & HIS SWEET HEART TIMMY. WHEN THE
MOMENT CAME & HIS MANI PINNED THE TWO STARS ON HIS
SHOULDERS. IT WAS ECSTACY. I WAS CHOCKED WITH EMOTIONS
& ALL THAT I COULD SAY IN THE HEAT OF THE MOMENT
WAS " I AM PROUD OF YOU MY SON - KEEP IT UP"
LET THIS MONTH OF JUN BE AUSPICIOUS FOR US. I GOT
MANI ON 8th JUN 74. YOU GOT COMMISSION ON 7 JUN 97 & ON
THIS DAY OF 8th JUN 74 YOU PROPOSED TO TIMMY. GOOD LUCK
                                                    - POPIN -

MESSAGE FROM A PROUD FATHER

Prof. S.K. Nayyar noted with pride the graduation of his son
from the Indian Military Academy, 7 June 1997.

WITH TIMMIE
The lieutenant on his engagement with his long-time girlfriend Timmie, 11 April 1998.

MR & MRS NAYYAR
Anuj's parents, on his engagement day.

SMILLING BROTHERS
Anuj with his younger sibling Karan.

ONE WITH THE JAWANS
The infamous letterman, January 1999. Anuj wrote home regularly from his postings.

Anuj and his men stretch their legs and unwind after a long day at
Chilling Heights, March 1999.

Anuj and his men atop a 13,000-feet peak, March 1999.

PROMOTION
Anuj Nayyar was promoted from the rank of lieutenant to captain at Kargil Heights, June 1999.

The Infantry School MHOW (M P)
YOUNG OFFICERS COURSE SERIAL - 87
09 Nov 98 to 03 Apr 99

Sitting L to R - Maj Vinay Khosla, Maj SK Rai, Maj SC Mann, Lt Col HV Sharma, Lt Col Bhatinder Singh, Col PC Chaudhary, Brig SK Trehan, Capt Pankaj Rana, Maj Gen JS Bhati, SM, Lt Gen DS Chauhan, UYSM, VSM, Breg LM Tewari, SM, VSM, Capt UPR Veerakoon, Col KS Aithani, Col PK Dhodapkar, Maj AR Deshpande, Maj R Bandhu, Maj R Manocha, Maj CS Dewgun, Capt AK Mishra.

Standing LtoR Maj VPS Kaushik, T Gilja, Lt Ram Prasad, BS Sidhu, Sudhir, KJ Sri Nivasan, Velu, Sunil, Sumer, R Bath, A Upadhaya, A Banga, P Parida, H Bansal, P Thapliyal, N Gehldt, A Nayyar, Parhik, G Ghuman, S Pujari, DK Basel, M Srivastav, Capt Charih, LtM Sakhawat, Capt S Agarwal.

1st Row

Standing LtoR 2 Lt KT Penjor, Lt Chaudhari, S Faentia, B Bhat, V Jondhale, SP Singh, J Chuba Sashi, KP Umrao, PS Saager, JV Singh, SN Guru, K Dasad, S Madan, D Gurung, TVK Satyanarayan, Rajesh Singh, G Sonal, Capt Rubern, Lt N Rajput, V Prasad, Shissh KP, Capt VDS Perera, Lt Vijay Rathi.

2nd Row

Standing LtoR Lt Kadam, Gayenka, S Rana, AP Singh, S Nimbalkar, YK Malik, Anil Kumar VR, R Ranjit, A Hoda, M Sangbora, P Surayan, S Bhatacharya, JB Chhetri, R Shekhar, P Modgili, Capt Jayasiri, Siri Wardhana, Pareea, Lt W Mexgo, Capt Paliekumbura, SB Amunugama, Lt Kishore.

3rd Row

Standing LtoR Lt Rajesh, BS Bhandari, SF Ahmad, R Mukundan, MS Kulkarni, Srijith, Arun, A Bhandari, A Yadav, S Saklani, Harpreet, A Das, PP Saha, Capt Anthony, Lt AB Bohara, P Shinde, V Vaidya, Y Singh, S Bahara, S jain, R Nanda, Vijay.

4th Row

Standing LtoR Lt RS Sekhon, R Kumar, H Dukpa, N Yadav, A Pawar, R Shinde, BS Khandka, B Gurung, R Mathew Kartikeya, AK Tiwari, S Mukherjee, BS Sawian, Tharchin, Wangdi, R Chaudri.

5th Row

YO'S-87

Anuj at the Young Officers Course, 3 April 1999.

HOISTING THE VICTORY FLAG

Mission accomplished by Capt. Anuj Nayyar and his men of 17 Jat at Pimple, 8 July 1999.

ANTIM PAG
The final steps in the young officer's journey – an army truck takes Capt. Anuj Nayyar
and his family to Brar Square Crematorium, 11 July 1999.

THE CAPTAIN'S LEGACY

Inauguration of 'Shaheed Captain Anuj Nayyar Sarvodaya Bal Vidyalaya',
Year 2000.

The Kargil Heights Filling Station, September 2021.

RASHTRIYA RIDERS

Team Rashtriya Riders visit Capt. Anuj Nayyar's mother in 2017, which later became a reason for this book.

GOLDEN NAME

Karan standing next to the plank bearing Capt. Anuj Nayyar's name at the Kargil War Memorial, August 2018

A rock that Karan got from Pimple 2, where his brother
breathed his last, on his visit to Kargil in 2018.

An artillery box from Kargil 1999 that Subedar Man
Singh presented to Karan on the trip to Pimple 2.

Text on memorial plaque:

CAPTAIN ANUJ NAYYAR
MAHA VIR CHAKRA (POSTHUMOUS)
17 JAT

On 06 July 1999, Charlie Company was tasked to capture an objective which was part of the Pimple Complex on the Western Slopes of Point 4875, in the Mushkoh Valley. When the Company Commander was injured, he took over command of the company and led the leading platoon of the company. As the platoon closed in, he killed three enemy personnel by firing a Rocket Launcher. During this act, an enemy RPG shell hit the officer, killing him on the spot. For displaying conspicuous courage in the face of enemy, he was posthumously awarded the Maha Vir Chakra.

THE ARMY PAYS HOMAGE
Capt. Anuj Nayyar on his martyrdom day at Kargil War Memorial, 7 July 2019.

When the Nayyars and Timmie finished packing the bag, no one could tell that it was meant for an army captain. From soft toys to chocolates, greeting cards to pickles, it was perhaps the most peculiar parcel for a conflict zone like Drass.

The bag that Anuj had packed stayed with him till the end of the Pimple Complex attack, even after he had breathed his last. And the bag from Delhi reached its destination twenty-four hours too late, on 8 July 1999. Anuj was already gone by then.

Back to the war, Maj. Rampal was still on hold requesting more ammunition to maintain the Whaleback post. Pimple 2 was yet to be captured and Point 4875 was still under enemy control.

After careful consideration, Col. Bawa planned to send Capt. Nayyar and Maj. Ritesh Sharma to the aid of Maj. Rampal. Anuj was instructed to carry maximum ammunition and provide support to the Delta Company until the position at Whaleback was secured. Anuj had one final realization before he went to the field that day – that he was not just a duty-bound, patriot of a soldier but also the protector of his fellow men. The decision had been made to start Anuj's fight a little earlier, at the call of his brothers in arms. The only job left was to let the men know what they had to do. Col. Bawa began to address his men with the seventeenth century *shabad* or hymn written by Guru Gobind Singh: '*Deh* Shiva *bar mohe.*'

O Lord Shiva, please bestow this blessing on me
That I never stray away from the path of righteous action,
I shall fight the enemy without any fear and ensure my victory.
May your glory be etched in my mind,
My only greed should be to speak about your virtues.
When this mortal life comes to end,
May I die fighting courageously on the battlefield.

The moment he heard his commander speak, Anuj knew that he was now at the *antim pag* or the final step that would change the destinies of many men. Later that evening, Anuj walked to the command tent of 17 Jat and handed a few things to Col. Bawa. He kept a watch and a leather wallet on Col. Bawa's table and said, 'Sir, in case I do not come back, please have these returned to my family.' After a pause, he told his commanding officer that he did not want to carry anything that would hold him back from taking necessary action in the battlefield, 'even if it means laying down my life'.

He then turned to 2IC Lt Col. Sharma, who was watching him from a corner of the tent, and said, 'Sir, please help Col. Bawa keep my engagement ring safe. That fiancée of mine won't spare me if I lose it in the field. I'll take these things from you if I return safely.' The CO tried to lighten the mood by saying, 'Why should you say so, Anuj? You'll come back, there's nothing up there that you can't handle. You'll win the peak, you'll come back safe, we'll all celebrate and Deepak (Maj. Rampal) has promised that he'll dance at your wedding. I wish you all the luck.'

Capt. Anuj Nayyar left the firebase of the Pimple Complex on the evening of 5 July. He was the leading platoon commander of the unit. Platoons 7, 8 and 9 of 17 Jat Battalion's Charlie Company were mobilized as reinforcements. One platoon was to reach Whaleback first and the other two were to support subsequent attacks on Pimple 2. The Charlie Company reached Whaleback to link-up with the Delta Company by 2130 hours. Maj. Rampal and his unit were down to their last cans by then. They had already repelled a counter-attack from the Pakistani side to recapture Whaleback.

Anuj revived the forces of the Delta Company and participated in the counter-attack, successfully staving off the second wave from the enemy side. Together Capt. Anuj and Maj. Rampal tackled the counter-attack from both sides of enemy fire while Maj. Ritesh Sharma covered them. By next morning the second wave was over, but another wave was mounting. Anuj and Sharma changed the positions of UMGs and MMGs to mitigate this attack while Anuj made calls to the firebase to calibrate the launchers. The final calibrations helped the Delta Company pound heavy cavalry on the incoming counter-attacks. Shells falling at the right positions broke the final wave.

Subedar Man Singh says Maj. Deepak Rampal and Capt. Anuj Nayyar made sure that Whaleback was completely secured by the end of 6 July. 'We were fighting back in broad daylight. Anuj sahab used to lead and cover for soldiers who fell back. And through the continuous firefight that lasted about eleven to thirteen hours, there were no more counter-attacks. We then decided to move to our primary task.'

As platoon commander, Capt. Nayyar gave the remaining necessary ammunition to Maj. Rampal and led the company to Pimple 2. The company started its move towards Pimple 2 at 2000 hours on 6 July and reached the peak's sentry post by 0230 hours the next day. Subedar Vinod Kumar says, 'Climbing the Pimple Complex was a fight by itself. For every fifty metres we would climb, we would slide back twenty-five metres. It was like quicksand, dragging us down, but Capt. Anuj kept calling the unit's battle cry "Jat Balwan, Jai Bhagwan" (The Jat is mighty, thank the lord.) We kept moving towards the post and then received instructions to delay the attack because day would break before we could complete our work at Pimple 2.'

As they waited for fresh instructions, Anuj checked on every member of the platoon to see if they had enough ammunition and food for the final ascent. 'Anuj sahab had a peculiar nature of tying all loose ends. His attack plans were most efficient, his patrol units meticulous in rationing. It is because of this habit that we had enough ammunition to take on Pimple 2,' says Subedar Vinod Kumar.

The platoon had barely moved a hundred metres from Whaleback when Anuj realized that Maj. Rampal may not have the required number of long-range weapons to handle a surprise attack. Despite knowing that a return trek might not be easy in the wee hours, Anuj still chose to carry UBL grenades, MMG magazines and UMG cans back to Maj. Rampal's base and came back to his company.

Halfway through Charlie Company's ascent towards the bunkers, they were met with heavy artillery, shelling, auto-fire and mortar shelling. The enemy had detected the company's movement, and had probably tried to establish contact with their colleagues at Pimple 1. By then that peak was under the control of Maj. R.K. Singh. Failure to make contact with Pimple 1 must have frustrated them to the extent that they increased shelling on Pimple 2. Maj. Sharma sustained an RPG (rocket-propelled grenade) splinter injury during this attack. The splinter rendered his leg non-functional. Five more men from the Charlie Company suffered critical injuries. As second in command, Capt. Anuj Nayyar collected the troops and took shelter while continuing the counter-attack on the first line of enemy defence at Pimple 2. Subedar Darshan, who was in charge of Platoon 7, was also immobilized by enemy shelling. Anuj informed Col. Bawa about the situation and suggested that Maj. Sharma be taken down by stretcher. The major, however, urged Anuj and the rest to move on.

Owing to Maj. Sharma's condition, Anuj was given full responsibility to lead the attack on Pimple 2. He was made the company commander of the Charlie Company by CO Col. Bawa. It was, quite literally, an uphill task, but Anuj did not flinch.

The company was already at a loss of leadership, the company commander had to be left behind and it was up to Anuj to lead the company and its men.

As soon as the Charlie Company reached the Pimple 2 sentry post, Anuj decided that the best way to go about would be in stealth mode. He was accompanied by NCOs Havildar Kumar, Havildar Hari Om, Havildar Bhagwan Singh and Sepoy Surendar Singh. He wanted to make sure that everyone in the attacking party remained as safe as possible and for as long as possible. So, he crawled up to the posts and reached within a fifty-metre-radius of the enemy's line of fire. He confirmed enemy positions by risking his own life and silenced them forever with his bayonet. The company continued to move and just when they were close enough to the first line of defence at Pimple 2, hidden Pakistani troops opened heavy fire on them.

Soon the place turned into a closed-combat arena with the infiltrators firing from every direction. According to Brig. Bawa, 'What worked well for Anuj was the kind of rapport he had built with the troops. They wouldn't have followed just anyone into the battle the way they did with Anuj.'

Capt. Nayyar ordered firebase support and even guided his men to hit the defence lines of the enemy. As the enemy fled to their bunkers from defence positions, he made sure that the unit and platoons were accounted for. The time had come for him to mount what has come to be known as one of the deadliest attacks of the Kargil war.

The Tiger of Drass was in no mood to spare the jackals. He was ready to wring their necks with his jaws. It was a fierce battle for territory. Over the next few hours, Anuj did what battalions would have taken days to accomplish. The men in those four bunkers on Pimple 2 must have realized they had messed with the wrong Indian.

As Anuj launched the attack on the first bunker with his rocket launcher, he figured that these were not just bunkers. They were fortresses chiselled in rocks. Each bunker was a part of a 'section guarded post', which means that independent artillery equipment at each bunker was capable of breaking any attack.

Subedar Vinod Kumar explains, 'Those were what we now call a sangar – a dome-shaped structure constructed from hollowed out boulder large enough to hold about fifteen men. It was impossible to identify the weak points of these bunkers in the dark.'

Capt. Nayyar then decided that continued attack with shoot-and-scoot movement (crouched and quickly switching positions) behind natural cover would be the best way to maximize effective fire radius for a direct assault. Many estimations can be made about how Pimple 2 could have been won silently, and without any loss of life. But all that is in the realm of conjecture. What actually transpired is the stuff of legends. Sepoy Surendar, being in the scout position of the platoon, took advantage of his proximity to the enemy. He reached close enough to the HMGs of the first bunker. With his bare hands, he pulled out the HMG barrels and gave his fellows some respite from non-stop firing.

The sepoy was in no mood to surrender even an inch of Indian territory to outsiders. He would have taken the bunker by himself but a hand grenade lobbed by an infiltrator led to his demise. In a fit of rage, Capt. Anuj and Havildar Hari Om charged to kill the enemies in that bunker. In close combat, they overpowered and killed two infiltrators at MMG positions using the *sangeen*, or a bayonet attached to the end of INSAS-SLR.

Realizing the threat to their positions, enemies at the other three bunkers intensified their attack. Subedar Man Singh recalls, 'Every shell dropping on us felt like it had passed through us. Every fifty metres we climbed felt like a mile. Anuj sir instructed two jawans to flank the enemy at the second bunker while he led the attack. He went ahead with Havildar Hari Om, while Havildar Kumar and Naik Rishipal hurled grenades inside enemy bunkers. The explosion gave the company enough cover to lead the all-out assault on the second bunker. The Charlie Company took control of it by killing three more opponents in hand-to-hand combat. It was only after they had secured the remaining positions in the bunker that the platoon came to know of the deaths of Havildar Kumar and Naik Rishipal.

The blitzkrieg that did not occur at Pimple 1 was coming to reality now. The hand-to-hand combat that was leading to these victories was almost poetic to Anuj's pre-war self. In a letter to his father, he had claimed that he had trained himself well in multiple weaponry systems and hand-to-hand combat. 'This brings me closer to being the soldier I want to become and the kind of soldier I want to be known as,' he wrote.

During the attack on the second bunker, Anuj refused to take cover or sit for even once, according to Subedar Vinod Kumar. 'It's not like he was being reckless; he made spot strategies, made better decisions and I sometimes reckon that if he hadn't been that way, we would probably be dead.'

Anuj was in a different state that day. Subedar Man Singh recalls him saying, 'I'm going to live very long, there's no bullet in Pakistan that could do me any harm today.' His jumps and leaps would resemble that of a young tiger. Soon, he would need all his might for the attack on the third bunker of Pimple 2.

The third bunker tested Anuj both mentally and physically. The shelling escalated the moment the Charlie Company started moving towards it. Subedar Vinod Kumar narrates, 'We were done with the second bunker by 0348 hours and the morning light had started to surface. It was then that the hiding sniper on Point 4875 started hitting our men. For fifteen whole minutes, we had no natural defence against him. In a series of assaults by artillery, auto-fire and sniper fire, the Charlie Company lost three more men and two soldiers were badly wounded.'

One of the men who died at that hour was the radio operator, who was hit by a mortar shell splinter. Anuj carried his lifeless body to a safe corner and lifted the radio set on to his back. It did not bother him that the radio set weighed almost twenty kilos.

The other soldiers followed Capt. Nayyar without a word. He decided to attack the third bunker despite the natural disadvantage of the rising sun. It was the only way to be safe from sniper fire.

They had barely moved from the spot where the radio operator had fallen when the infiltrators on nearby peaks started artillery shelling on Pimple 2 to back up their men trapped there. In the next two to three minutes, a barrage of continuous shelling by both NLI firebase and artillery unit descended on the men of 17 Jat Battalion. By then the silence of the operation had already been disrupted. And thus started the chants of the war cry: Jat Balwan, Jai Bhagwan!

Havildar Hari Om interrupted his captain, looking for confirmation that they were moving in for the kill. But to expect an ounce of doubt from Anuj was like finding a safe spot in the face of enemy fire. Subedar Vinod Kumar exclaims, 'When the tiger had his prey in sight, how could he have stopped!' Subedar Man Singh recalls that the enemy had started pelting the Indian soldiers with just about anything they could lay their hands on, from empty shells to stones. 'At that height, even a ten-gram stone pellet could hit us at fifty miles an hour, but we carried on. Anuj sahab led the team from at the front. As we reached the firing location for the third bunker, Maj. Punia wanted to talk to Anuj about the status of the operation,' the subedar says.

While he was on the call with Maj. Punia, a mortar shell landed just inches away from the platoon position. And then the deadly firing from the third bunker began. The enemy knew that Anuj's team was close. Continued firing from both sides was proving futile. No one was able to move an inch forward and daylight was blowing the cover of the Indian troops.

In a swift decision, one of the men tried to take a direct shot at the bunker with a rocket launcher. However, owing to the intricate make of the bunker and the distance to it, an accurate shot was very difficult. After a failed attempt, Capt. Nayyar took over the weapon and launched another shot which went through a small opening and inflicted serious damage on the target.

The company continued crawling towards the third bunker through mud and smoke. It was then that Naib Subedar Virendar Singh's SLR got stuck. Anuj noticed this and wasted no time in throwing his AK-47 to Singh. 'He knew that the AK-47 was a better assault weapon in his hands, much more than mine. Still, he gave me his weapon in the blink of an eye,' recalls the soldier. Anuj had no time to judge the qualities of the gun; it was time to trust in the qualities of the men at his side.

Anuj continued to support the team with his calls, instructions and war cries. Simultaneously, the Pakistani sniper which the Indian forward troops had missed in a battle on another peak was taking potshots at Indian soldiers while they were busy fighting. Minutes later, Havildar Kumar fell to the bullets of this sniper. Capt. Nayyar then decided to ditch an organized approach towards the enemy. Incidentally, the sniper in question was later killed in action by the mopping up party of 2 Naga, following the operations at Point 4875. Continuing their assault, to silence the MMG post at this bunker, Anuj crawled ahead of the unit and sneaked right below it. Then with his bare hands he held the barrel of the enemy MMG and pulled it out to neutralize the post for good.

After beating an MMG post, Anuj tried throwing in a couple of hand grenades, which went in vain. The sangar was too strong. Anuj went ahead with one more soldier and dropped a grenade right inside the bunker. That was the end of it. Now all that was between Anuj and total victory was the final bunker of Pimple 2.

The men in the fourth bunker may have bitten their tongue on seeing a boyish-looking soldier at their threshold. Seeing Anuj race towards the final bunker, Subedar Man Singh thought of the young officer's upcoming marriage. 'He was moving so fast and fearlessly, it seemed his marriage was scheduled for the next day,' he laughs drily. But Anuj had a deadline to keep: deliver Pimple 2 to his seniors by 0500 hrs.

'Anuj sir gathered the remaining soldiers and motivated them to launch the attack on the last bunker. We would be remembered for the service to our country and we would be remembered as people who stoked fear in the hearts of Pakistanis. So, Anuj sir told us that he was sure each one of us would be there standing in those bunkers, proudly hoisting the Indian flag.' After the pep talk, the Jats rose as a pack with the war cry of their regiment.

With a limited yet motivated unit, Anuj led the teams to the fourth bunker. Under the instructions of Col. Bawa, he was not to disrupt the mission at any point for repeated intel and was to only make contact for any emergency, evaluation, support or suggestion.

At the fourth bunker shelling from the Indian firebase had stopped. Anuj began with the regular approach of targeted firing and periodic shelling combined with grenades and rocket launchers. But that did not even scratch the bunker.

Anuj decided that they needed a breakthrough and went straight for the loopholes of the enemy bunker. He tried to throw live grenades inside. It almost felt like he was back in the academy where life was competition and defeat was something he could not afford. Anything that had even a small chance of diluting the enemy's advantage was important. He also reverse-threw hand grenades but none made it inside the bunker. The loophole was cut to the size of a gun barrel and nothing more.

Anuj then launched the last of his rockets with the assistance of Sepoy Virender Kumar. But the rocket bounced off the structure. It was almost like the sangar was damage repellent.

There was constant altercation, too, between the enemy and Anuj. He asked his men to sever two communication lines belonging to the opponent, in order to prevent any calls for enemy reinforcements and the possibility of artillery shelling from the other side.

It was getting closer to the reporting time and efforts were not bearing fruit. Some men suggested that Anuj call for back-up while they held their positions. Anuj knew that staying at their positions in broad daylight would not only expose them to the enemy units at Pimple 2 but also the enemy sniper on another peak. He knew he had to rely on stealth and risky ascent for a breakthrough.

But before he could start, he waited a moment at the side of a rock. He probably remembered his father reading the names of war heroes and award winners at the IMA hall and saying, '*Yaar*, Anuj, *iss mein ek bhi* Nayyar *nahin hain?*' He must have felt like looking at his family once more. As he slid his hand in his pocket to pull out his wallet, he remembered that he had left it with Col. Bawa. He then took out a cigarette and lit it up. He smiled as he took a long drag of the cigarette. Mani did not know that he smoked and probably more times in a day than she could accept. Subedar Subhash Singh, who was next to him, says, 'I saw him smiling with a faraway look on his face, like he was deep in thought. He broke from his thoughts and knew that it was time for the final assault. He made the decision to let go of his safety if he had to end this battle. He was now fiercer than ever. Taking shelter and the original scoot-and-shoot plan was no longer an option. He stood as a single line of defence between his men and the enemy. His was the stand of a tiger amidst the barrage of bullets and grenades.

Subedar Subhash realized the risk his commander was taking to ensure the end of the battle. He urged him to take shelter for his own safety. Capt. Anuj's immediate response was, 'Subhash, *yeh dekh mera haath, yeh* lifeline *dekh*. Dad *kehte hain ki yeh bahut lambi hain. Mujhe kuchh nahin ho sakta hain.*' (Subhash, look at my hand, look at this lifeline. My father says that it's very long. Nothing can harm me.)

Still, Subedar Subhash pulled his captain's hand to make sure that he took shelter from enemy fire. Anuj took this moment to reassess the situation with his team. His radio set buzzed, and it was Col. Bawa on the other side. Anuj straightened up a bit and told his commanding officer about the attack mounted on the last bunker and how they were left with little ammunition. But at no point did he ask for more support.

Brig. Bawa remembers telling him that reinforcements were not an option. Anuj replied, 'Sir, three down, one to go. Don't you worry, sir, I'll have that peak for you in just some time. I'll myself ...' and the line went dead.

It was 0520 hours. Brig. Bawa kept calling Anuj to see if there had been a disruption in the line. He had heard a loud noise but got no response from the other end. He kept asking for a situation report, but received no reply. There in the peaks of Drass, at some 16,000 feet, Subedar Subhash and the other men could not believe what had just happened. 'We remember an RPG coming towards us. We remember the explosion. For a moment we thought that we had lost our lives,' narrates the survivor. As the men recovered from the explosion they realized that their commander had saved their lives.

A rocket-propelled grenade had gone straight through his neck and pierced him through the length of his chest and torso – ending the life but not the spirit of the young captain. The soldiers still believe that Anuj saved fifteen lives by taking on that RPG. It took but a moment of the war to turn the tide with his sacrifice. He was motivating his men in life, and he was motivating them even more in his death.

Seeing this, Havildar Hari Om could not stop himself. He charged at the enemy with all his rage and killed two of them before he fell lifeless next to his captain.

The young officer had entered the battlefield, which was no less than the chakravyuha, the tactical maze described in Mahabharata, like Abhimanyu. Brig. Bawa is full of glowing praise as he remembers Anuj – 'He did way better than what we could have expected from anyone. He fought like a true Jat and Indian. I feel proud to have served by such an officer and jewel of the country.'

Captain Anuj Nayyar's was a life of transformation, from the lanes of Janakpuri to the corridors of Chetwode Hall, IMA, and the bunk beds of Naushera Company to the ranks of the Jat Regiment, a life of code and honour, of friendships and family, ambition and loyalty, rules and patriotism, *josh* and resilience, a life of *izzat* and a life of sacrifice – and he had been delivered to the eternal flame of martyrs, the Amar Jawan Jyoti.

The war did not stop, though. By the time the soldiers got back to their senses, the enemy had started a full-scale attack on the Charlie Company. Subedar Man Singh says, 'We didn't panic when we saw others dying in the line of duty; they were good, honourable men. But to find our leader lying dead in front of our eyes filled us with rage. An officer far younger than us had shown us the meaning of courage and the enemy was still trying to press advantage.'

Capt. Shashi Bhushan Ghidiyal, an artillery officer deployed as forward observation officer with 17 Jat, took charge in Capt. Nayyar's stead and marched towards the enemy.

'Such was the anger and vengefulness that we could have been as inhuman to the enemy as they had been to us and to our captain. The remaining ten or twelve members of Charlie Company continued a brute force attack. But nothing was able to bring back Capt. Anuj Nayyar or any of our friends we had lost,' recalls Subedar Man Singh.

Despite continued efforts to link-up with the Charlie Company, the men of the Bravo Company were not able to come through the heavy firing from the fourth bunker and Point 4875. To prevent further casualties, the Charlie Company was instructed to hold off any assault until dark. When artillery was in a position to support the Pimple Complex once again at 2000 hours, Capt. Ghildiyal launched an artillery and mortar assault on the remaining infiltrators. They had to leave their attack positions and take shelter in the sangars of Pimple 2. Later that night, a joint attack from Pimple 1, Whaleback and the battalion firebase was initiated to smoke them out. The attack continued all night without any credible outcome.

The built of the sangars and the topography on which they were located protected them from any projectile.

In the early morning hours of 8 July 1999, the enemy had thought of escaping the continuous onslaught of artillery, mortar and bullets when Maj. R.K. Singh of the Alpha Company noticed them and shot two of the four men before they could run back to the safety of Point 4875. In succession, the Delta Company under Maj. Rampal and the men of the Alpha Company managed to search and annihilate the remaining infiltrators from the Pimple Complex.

The men of 17 Jat had done their bit to save the country. *Naam, namak, nishaan* (name, fealty, mark) – Capt. Anuj Nayyar and his men had lived by these three principles of a soldier's life. The unit was awarded forty-one bravery awards for their operation on Pimple 1, Whaleback and the treacherous Pimple 2, which later paved the way for the successful capture of important peaks. Capt. Anuj Nayyar was posthumously awarded the Maha Vir Chakra, which turns out to be one of the highest gallantry awards in the Jat Regiment's history.

At 0718 hours on 8 July, the Indian national flag was hoisted at the Pimple Complex by the Indian armed forces, 79 Infantry Brigade and 17 Jat Battalion. Capt. Anuj Nayyar may not have been there that morning but he was present in the victorious soldiers who basked in his glory.

'White on Walls and White off Walls'

Capt. Anuj Nayyar had done a great service in leading his men to the last point of the Pimple Complex and delivering the key feature of Pimple 2. The victory of Pimple 2 is what rid Tiger Hill of threats from its western flanks. It also helped resume traffic on NH1A from Ghumri to Zoji La, with trucks bringing on-time supply of ammunition and ration to military bases. Another battle was fought the same day at Peak 4875, now known as Batra Top. At about 1300 hours, when a fierce counter-attack was being charged on the final machine gun posts of Point 4875, the victory of Pimple 2 and by extension the Pimple Complex ensured there were no reinforcements for the Pakistanis facing the ire of Capt. Vikram Batra's AK-47. By the end of the following week, the entire Drass sector was purged of enemy forces.

At 0543 hours of 7 July, when Col. Bawa was not getting any news of Anuj and the location of the Charlie Company, he made contact with Maj. Punia at Pimple 1, who was asked to link up with Anuj and update the commanding officer.

When Maj. Punia established contact with the Charlie Company at Pimple 2, he got to know of Anuj and his men's bravery. He found the survivors in a state of shock, waiting for someone to jolt them back to reality. He used the radio to call CO Bawa and said, 'I am sorry, sir, but Anuj is no more ...'

Second in command Lt Col. Sharma was with the commanding officer when he got call. He did not know how to react to the news: 'I was silent for a few minutes as he (Maj. Punia) described how Anuj had led the men to victory. After that, I had no idea what he was saying ... I was engulfed by the grief of losing the youngest officer I had sent to the front. My victories had gone sour with the loss of my soldiers but I was simply unable to accept Anuj's demise. This was the peak he was supposed to gift me on my birthday. He did deliver on his promise but not in person.'

Battalion adjutant Maj. Madan, too, was in the command tent when Maj. Punia reported the events at Pimple 2. After the call, all three officers stood staring at each other quietly. It was time to break the news to his family. Col. Bawa declined the unenviable task of informing Anuj's parents. He said he would not be able to control his emotions because of his closeness to the Nayyars. Finally, Lt Col. Sharma made the call.

Sharma remembers, 'I had to gulp down my sorrow and make sure that the news was delivered in the most honourable way to his family. His family had to be assured that many would shudder to even think of what the brave captain had done for the country. A part of my conscience was disturbed by the thought that we had failed to do our duty towards Anuj while he had done every bit of his. It's always hard choosing one's words while informing a fallen soldier's family of "the news".'

The only thing that the Nayyars did those days was watch TV news channels and pray for Anuj's safety. Timmie would stay over sometimes to be with Mani and Prof. Nayyar.

Mani remembers her husband reading Anuj's letters over and over again. 'In his last letter, which he wrote on 29 June, Anuj asked his father to not worry about the money for the car they had planned to buy together. Prof. Nayyar had shown me that letter some ten times. He took pride in knowing that he had raised a son who knew his duties both to the nation and to the family,' she says.

The father would then read the letter sent earlier that month, none of which talked about his posting in the war zone. 'Had it not been for the commendations, we would never know what exactly happened to my son. I know it's not true but that's how the news of your son's sacrifice hits you,' says Mani.

Going back to the morning of Lt Sharma's call, Mani recalls it being unpleasantly warm. Prof. Nayyar was sipping his tea, and she was complaining about the heat. 'It was like any other Wednesday morning, except that our son was in the war zone where two hostile countries were in high-altitude combat,' the mother describes.

Mani had just asked her husband to apply for a car loan for Anuj.

Prof. Nayyar had quipped, 'I will. I am just waiting for him to give me a colour preference.'

Mani looked around the house for Naughty, their pet dog who gave them company at tea every morning. 'Where's Naughty?' she asked.

Naughty was nowhere to be found. Not even behind the sofa where he liked to scratch his back. Mani urged the professor to search for the dog inside the residential complex where they lived. She had a bad feeling about this. She had got the dog to keep everyone in the family safe – its disappearance was surely a bad omen. Naughty was finally found at a neighbourhood park. With the dog secured, the Nayyar couple was able to get on with their day and prepared to leave for work.

At about 9.15 a.m., the phone rang. Mani was about to receive the call but the professor beat her to it. 'Sometimes I wonder if Anuj had told him about the big operation at the Pimple Complex and Prof. Nayyar knew a phone call that early, on the day that Anuj was supposed to capture the peak, could either be only good or very, very bad,' says Mani.

On the other end of the phone, Lt Col. Sharma held his breath till he heard Anuj's father's voice. 'I was praying to god that it be Anuj's father on the line. I didn't have the courage to break the news to his mother or his brother. This is not something that the army trains you for. This notion that is the bedrock of the army's courage – that we are invincible, that we are undefeated. And it makes us unwary to the idea that we are mortals. I was not prepared but Prof. Nayyar's voice gave me courage. Anuj's father spoke with dignity and respect.'

As Lt Col. Sharma introduced himself, Prof. Nayyar asked the dreaded question: 'Is it about Anuj?'

Lt Col. Sharma replied, 'Yes, sir. I'm sorry to inform you that while doing a great service for the nation today, we lost Anuj this morning at 0530 hrs.'

There was complete silence. And then there was a gentle sob. 'Did he die fighting?' asked the father.

Lt Col. Sharma immediately knew all that Anuj stood for came from his father. Even at this hour of grief, Prof. Nayyar was concerned about his son's duty to the nation.

'Indeed, he did. A glorious fight, worthy of immortal praise,' said the lieutenant colonel.

He then gave him the details of how Anuj had saved the lives of nearly fifteen men, killed nine infiltrators and delivered the peak that would symbolize the victory of the Indian Army. 'It was unnatural to give him technical details when I should've been consoling him,' says Lt Col. Sharma, 'but I felt compelled to explain why we had failed to take care of his son and why he had to die while we survived.'

Standing next to her husband, Mani watched the man go numb. 'He was absolutely still. Breathless and motionless. I could see anger in his eyes and exhaustion on his face. He was grieving but he was angrier.'

Prof. Nayyar put the receiver down as Karan and Mani watched him breathlessly. It was supposed to be just another day for, who was planning to catch a movie with his friends. But the phone call changed everything.

'I picked up the phone. Though the voice of the caller was barely audible, I was able to make out some words. "Operation", "hospital", "killed in action" ... That was enough for me. Even I froze for a moment and just put the receiver down. I couldn't grasp any information being delivered to me. I'd lost the only anchor I had in my life,' Karan says.

Over the next few hours, Mani informed relatives that Anuj was missing in action in Kargil. The real news would have been hard on many of them who were travelling to be with the family.

Anuj's elder uncle, Ashish, Timmie and her parents, Anuj's maternal aunts, his friends and some army officials gathered in the house. Mani wept inconsolably while Timmie tried to calm her. But it was Prof. Nayyar that everyone was worried about. He had not shed a tear or spoken a word.

Prof. Nayyar could be seen in empty corners of the house. His isolation was not just about guarding his emotions. He did not want to appear vulnerable and attract undue attention from anyone who did not know the Nayyar family.

After a statement to the press that was eager to know about Anuj's 'homecoming', and one which left the father seething, Prof. Nayyar punched a wall.

Karan ran to his father. It took both Karan and Mani to control his anger. When asked later, he confessed that he was angered by the shameful dismissal of facts and the plight of Indian soldiers by the Pakistan Army Chief Pervez Musharraf.

This outburst, no matter how much it hurt him, freed the family from the hatred and anger of the moment. A minute later, the professor was helping the neighbourhood children with water, his hand bound by a kerchief.

In the next room, Mani and close family members consoled each other. Karan sat in a corner holding on to the one photo of him and his brother in front of a boxing ring at the IMA. All he wanted at that moment was his brother, scolding him for not listening to Mani, encouraging him to exercise more, or refusing to share the bike with him.

Anuj's maternal aunt remembers the last conversation with her favourite nephew just one week prior to his death: 'He was all chirpy and told me that he was going on a big mission.' She worried about him but he sounded fearless. He had said, 'It's not going to be a hard mission. Just crash-and-burn stuff!'

His last request to her was to take care of his mother and to tell her not to worry.

The silence in the house, despite the huge number of people who had gathered there, was broken by an occasional sob or the sound of a TV news channel.

Suddenly Prof. Nayyar stormed into the drawing room where everyone was sitting.

As grief-struck as he was, there was somehow a strength in him that everyone needed at that moment. He declared in an authoritative voice: 'Please stop crying, I will not have anyone tarnish the memory of my brave son.'

Everyone was silent; Prof. Nayyar was brimming with anger. Anuj used to say, 'Poppin can do anything. There are things that I'd shy away from but not Poppin.' And that's what the father did. His stern but reasonable attitude reminded Karan of Anuj. By then, news channels had started announcing that Capt. Anuj Nayyar was being nominated for the Param Vir Chakra, India's highest gallantry award for acts of bravery during wartime, by his unit. In his recommendation letter, Anuj's commanding officer wrote that he 'acted beyond the call of duty with exemplary courage and determination and made the supreme sacrifice in the highest traditions of the regiment and the Indian Army. Captain Anuj Nayyar is strongly recommended for the Param Vir Chakra (Posthumous)'.

Prof. Nayyar shifted in his seat and switched off the television.

Mani says, 'We didn't need the commendation or the medal. What we needed was our son. I wanted those culprits who had let the terrorists cross the border punished in the first place. I wanted someone to bring my son back. When you realize that the love you've nurtured for the better part of your life is gone forever, no reasoning seems to work. I'm still not at peace, and I might never be,' Mani breaks down as she says this.

In the next few days, various government officials, army officers and politicians visited the family. Every time a politician would come over, their security team would sweep the whole residential complex for threats. 'It used to enrage me,' says Mani, 'their audacity to check before coming to a martyr's home, to rank their lives higher than those soldiers whom they had sent to the hills with partial information. Their lives held more value but the lives of those who ensured their safety were expendable.' Prof. Nayyar was more in control in these situations. 'My blunt dismissal of their visits was evident, but he kept it together.'

The night before Anuj's arrival at the Delhi air base, Karan and Mani sat together as they watched a stream of visitors drop by. When some army officials came to meet Prof. Nayyar, the mother and son drew the curtains for a moment of privacy and conversation.

Karan said to his mother then, 'Mani, *yeh jo kuchh bhi bacha hain ab aap hi sambhal sakte ho. Main jaanta hoon* (I know that you're the only one who can hold things together in these times). For Anuj's sake, you have to be strong now. For Anuj Bhai, for Dad and for everyone else.'

Mani says, 'Karan helped me realize that now I had to create a future for this family. His words still ring in my ears every time I stand by the name plate of Maha Vir Shaheed Captain Anuj Nayyar. I had but one duty now – to hold this family together in the living memory of Anuj.'

On 10 July, Prof. Nayyar received Anuj at the Delhi Cantonment after he was flown in from the Hindon air base. Anuj's uncle and Timmi's father went in for identification.

Among those who had come to be with the family – army officials, friends, family, neighbours – there were some unkind voices. Some were not there to help a father grieve, or console a weeping mother. All they wanted was firsthand details from the battlefield. They were news diggers disguised as mourners, asking questions such as, did he capture the peak? Did he die fighting? Was no one else available? Did he lose his post? But the family was grateful to those who helped them through these tough times.

A member of the Legislative Assembly visited the family to pay his condolences.

Every caller had the same question: 'When will the body come?' He, too, was no different.

'I used to implore them to not call Anuj "a body". They could've called him Captain, Anuj or anything else but reducing his being to just a body was unacceptable,' his mother recalls of the time. Prof. Jagdish Mukhi was among the first ones to ask the right question: 'When are they bringing your son back?' He came to the cremation and laid the wreath over Capt. Anuj Nayyar's pyre.

Sonia Gandhi, too, was decorous while meeting the family. But no one could answer Mani's simple questions: 'Why did our children have to mount this war? Why was there was no oversight at the border patrolling? Why were the Pakistani forces allowed to penetrate so deep inside Indian territories?'

The next day, Anuj's mortal remains in a coffin draped with the Indian national flag were placed in the middle of Central Park, BE Block, Janakpuri. The Nayyar residence and their housing complex had been flooded with people from 7 to 10 July. On 11 July, roads in the neighbourhood were jammed as people came out in hundreds to pay homage to the brave soldier.

Capt. Anuj Nayyar's wreath-laying ceremony was done in that park. While Mani sat and lay her head on Anuj's coffin, Prof. Nayyar put on a brave face, not shedding a tear, not talking to anyone and not showing any expression of loss. Karan says, 'In his last phone call with Anuj Bhai, Poppin gave him three suggestions, which, perhaps, became his commandments in the war: do not turn your back on the enemy, do not get captured, and win and come back.'

When the army's Tatra truck, decorated with flowers, came in to take Anuj on his final journey, the crowd chanted 'Anuj Nayyar *amar rahe*' (long live Anuj Nayyar). Prof. Nayyar, Karan, Ashish and his uncle lifted Anuj's coffin and took it to the truck to place it in open view of the visitors. For about eight kilometres, starting from Janakpuri to Brar Square Crematorium, the cortège of Shaheed Anuj Nayyar included university students, army officials, senior citizens and commoners; there was not a second when the chants died down. In the crowd, there were some 17 Jat soldiers and officials and they raised the call of their regiment: 'Jat Balwan, Jai Bhagwan'. When but a few voices raised to complete the war cry, Prof. Nayyar joined in, and others followed soon after. This was the motto by which Capt. Anuj Nayyar had achieved greatness, this was the motto to which he had dedicated the last days of his life.

Capt. Anuj Nayyar was not just a soldier who had died on the battlefield. He was the embodiment of the Indian people. Anuj was only twenty-three years old; the men and women, the soldiers and officers in the procession had sons older than him while some of them were themselves the same age. By the time the army truck reached the crematorium, thousands had gathered behind it.

The last rites of the Indian Army with full military honour started with the 'Last Post' bugle call played by a group of soldiers and a guard of honour for Capt. Anuj Nayyar. Karan lit the funeral pyre. Before the deceased captain was interred in Brar Square Crematorium, Karan wanted to make sure his brother had come back whole, if not alive. He felt each end of Anuj's arms and feet to check.

As the Nayyars collected Anuj's ashes, it became clear that their existence had been reduced to a singularity. Anuj's family might have had different aspirations, routines and thoughts, but now their life was going to revolve around Anuj's image and his honour.

Mani says, 'For a moment, we had forgotten that his sacrifice had a value separate from his loss to the family. It is hard for parents to realize that. Anuj had given his life for an idea that he felt was greater than all of us, greater than his own life. He had gone up there with the expectation that we would understand and accept his decisions, his drive and his sacrifice.'

On the fourth day after the cremation, a prayer meeting was held at the BE Block Central Park. Tents were set up and water was arranged. In the scorching heat of July, volunteers from the crowd managed the steady flow of visitors. While Anuj's parents were in mourning, it was a self-serving communion of concerned citizens who mourned with them by serving them in any way possible.

The parents did not know who had set up the tents or who had arranged for the water, barricades, generators and fans. After the prayer meeting, Prof. Nayyar went over to the local shops to make payments for the service but everything had already been paid for. On the tenth day after the last rites, Anuj's ashes were immersed in the Ganga at Haridwar; the priests refused to accept money for the rites. They said that in ancient times, warriors were accorded the highest honour. Their last rites were performed by the high priests. It was an honour for them to do the same for the warrior who had laid down his life in Kargil. 'They even cited the Bhagavad Gita to say that souls like Anuj's reach heaven without any pandit,' Mani remembers with a small smile.

Later, reporters visited the Nayyars for interviews and politicians came to console the bereaved family. Prof. Nayyar and Mani were so devastated by the loss that they both had confined themselves in their house. Karan went back to his preparations for engineering exams. Prof. Nayyar would go out occasionally to escape the walls of their home that echoed with Anuj's laughter. He would walk by the park, visit Anuj's school and return home after hours. He would also sit by Anuj's mother who could still feel his baby steps around the house. Their grief, though united by their love for Anuj, was different. One had lost a brother in arms, a confidante, an alter ego while the other had lost a part of herself, the meaning of her existence.

A few days later, Anuj's parents got the confirmation letter for the Maha Vir Chakra. Any award by the Indian government or military honour was small in comparison to his service.

The family received many letters, most offering condolences, while some praised Anuj's life. Some of them even shared stories which the Nayyars did not know about and were overwhelmed by the outpouring of love from his friends and colleagues. Subedar Virendar Singh from 17 Jat remembers the leader 'who kept giving us everything that ensured the victory that night. He shared his rifle, he went ahead of us to ensure our safety, he fought on the front line, took over the responsibilities which weren't assigned to him but were worthy of only a great officer. In his last breath, he gave us his life and the peak.'

On 11 April 2000, Prof. S.K. Nayyar received the Maha Vir Chakra for his son, Capt. Anuj Nayyar. Mani and Karan accompanied him to the Rashtrapati Bhavan where other families of war heroes were also present. 'It was overwhelming to see the families who had lost their child to the inhuman and unwanted war. My son Anuj and many other young men could've been in these halls receiving their rightful honour that day. I could not speak the whole time I was there. There were mothers of third-generation armymen and second-generation war heroes. There were widows, some twenty–twenty-five years old. There was more white off the walls than on it.'

After the Param Vir Chakra awards were conferred on war heroes Gdr. Yogendra Singh Yadav (18 Grenadiers), Capt. Manoj Kumar Pandey (1/11 Gorkha Rifles), Capt. Vikram Batra (13 Jammu and Kashmir Rifles) and Rifleman Sanjay Kumar (13 Jammu and Kashmir Rifles), Anuj's father was called to the stage. He walked up to the centre of the hall as the war citation for his son was read out.

After this, Prof. Nayyar was supposed to walk up to President K.R. Narayanan to receive the medal. Hearing how his son had given his life made him pause. His son had undergone a divine transformation – he was now a story, a legend. And to his father, a memory. The honours board of martyrs in Indian wars at the National Defence Academy now had a Nayyar among those brave names.

As he reached the stage and the president handed the medal to him, Prof. Nayyar realized the weight Anuj had left him with. The medal felt heavy in his hand, but he could lift it because he was empowered by the deed of his son. From now on, he would have the honour of being known as the father of Kargil war hero and Maha Vir Chakra recipient, Shaheed Captain Anuj Nayyar.

5

The Second War

FOR THE NEXT FIFTEEN YEARS after his death, the family chose to lock away his memories. Mani and Poppin put away his books, files, certificates, photos, medals and insignias neatly in closets and folders. It was too painful to be reminded of his absence every time they came across any of his belongings. It was only when this book was first conceived that the family unlocked all his possessions.

Within the four walls of the house, Anuj's parents and brother led a quiet, secluded life. Prof. Nayyar stopped going to the consulting firm that Anuj had inaugurated with him. When he was posted in the Kashmir Valley, the young officer encouraged his father to try out new things. The consulting firm was one such venture. Mani lost her appetite and spent long hours in silence by herself. She stopped answering phone calls or receiving visitors. Once in a while, the Nayyars stepped out for an evening stroll in the park.

Mani would spend hours sitting quietly on park benches or in her library office. She was in a state of suspended animation, running loops of her time with Anuj. Neighbours, bystanders and colleagues at the library would often notice her lost in thought and talk to her. Though they wished to console her, they would end up talking about Anuj. Prof. Nayyar, Karan and her relatives were her anchor in such times, and would try to keep her pain at bay.

Mani would often wonder how Anuj carried out his last mission on an empty stomach. He had wanted to eat something before going to the peaks, and all he had were some biscuits and frozen puris. Anuj dying without a hearty meal was something his mother could not accept. Ever since then, she makes sure that anyone who comes to the Nayyar residence is fed well before they leave.

While Mani had work to distract her and Karan had college, Poppin was still trying to find ways to occupy his time. He had stopped going to the consultancy office altogether, so Mani decided it was time to intervene. She purposefully moved he computer to his office. He needed a distraction, she reasoned. It was during those days that Prof. Nayyar wrote a couple of books on international finance management, dedicating them all to his son. He also wrote a few poems for Anuj during this period.

The Nayyars were overwhelmed by the avalanche of condolence messages and calls. Mani in particular had stopped attending calls from army officials and the media. One morning, soon after Anuj's death, her phone rang. She handed it to her husband. 'There was a strange sadness in his voice as he spoke to the caller,' she recalls. After a pause, the visibly emotional father said that a bag the family had packed for Anuj had reached the army base and the unit awaited instructions on what do with the parcel. Prof. Nayyar instructed that the sweets and pickles Mani had prepared for her soldier son be distributed among his colleagues who were still posted in Kashmir. The family knew that Anuj would have been happy to see his platoon enjoy the goodies.

His resident trunk was delivered to the family by two armymen in the coming days. Most of it came back directly from the war front bearing signs of his tryst with the enemy. It had his muddy boots, uniform, wallet and his engagement ring that was guarded by Brig. Bawa. 'We were receiving tokens with which we would remember him for eternity.' The trunk also included Anuj's personal belongings like unsent letters, diaries and notebooks, water bottle and books. 'I could see Anuj sitting by the door where the armymen placed the trunk. But what does a parent say to the person who has come to her with her dead child's belongings?' asks the mother wistfully.

Mani was lost in her thoughts so the professor, standing behind her, asked the armymen to come in. As they did, Mani felt as if Anuj had returned to them. She could feel his presence in the house, as if his life had come a full circle. Anuj had come back to where it all started. From an army officer to an NDA cadet and back to his childhood days when he used to walk around the house wearing an anklet.

For Prof. Nayyar it was a right day out of his worst nightmare. Once when Anuj had come home on mid-term leave from Mhow and his bags had to be brought back to Delhi as he stayed on for jaundice treatment, he had hesitated to bring home a soldier's bag without the soldier. He knew what it meant for the families of armymen. And it had happened to him. His son's trunk had returned without his son and there was nothing he could do about it.

In the following days, the Nayyars found solace in the company of soldiers recovering at the Army Base Hospital in Delhi. They visited with them and brought them sweets and gifts. Mani also resumed work at the library. Mani, Poppin and Karan found their own ways of mourning Anuj and coping with his loss. In the evenings, the three would come together in the house to mend each other's wounds. None of them wanted to be home alone alone with Anuj's memories – so they adjusted their schedules accordingly. Maybe that is what kept them going.

Mani took time out to meet soldiers who had been rescued from Kargil. Some of them were from her son's unit. Over the next two years, she sought refuge in the words of appreciation and anecdotes from soldiers who had met and worked with Anuj. Even the silence of other bereaved families was more comforting than any gallantry award or compensation.

Among those who visited the Nayyars was Col. Paresh Gupta, a close friend of Anuj. 'I was posted in Dehradun at the time and my company was awaiting instructions for deployment in Kargil. One day I came across a news report on Anuj being nominated for the Maha Vir Chakra,' he says.

He decided to call Timmie with the news. 'But the moment I heard her voice, I knew there was nothing I could say to make her feel better. I stammered for a while before breaking down. She consoled me,' Col. Gupta says, likening her courage to that shown by Anuj.

In November 1999, Col. Gupta came to Delhi for a language course before his next posting. He went to meet Anuj's parents on Timmie's suggestion. It was not their first meeting. The Nayyars had met him several times during their son's academy days. 'All that I wanted to tell Prof. Nayyar didn't come to my lips. I just stood silently in front of him,' says Col. Gupta. After a few moments of silence, he finally managed to mumble, 'Uncle, I can't seem to find the right words … I am sorry.'

'You don't need to say anything. Just sit beside me,' the professor replied. 'With you here, it feels like Anuj is here,' he added.

Since that meeting, Col. Gupta made it a point to visit the Nayyars as often as he could, mostly on Saturdays. He would have meals with the family, discuss business with Prof. Nayyar and even accompany them on walks in the neighbourhood park. Timmie would also join them at times.

Col. Gupta says Mani did not speak much those days. She would sit quietly in a corner or just go about her daily chores. Karan's pain was less accounted for. Between his mother's grief and his father's brave attempts at getting life back on track, he did not get enough time to process his own loss. His life, too, had taken a huge hit. He was most worried for his father, who did not let him or anyone in on his sorrow. It was the professor's way of keeping Karan focused on his career. But he wanted to share his father's pain, not just his dreams.

In March 2000, the Nayyars received a letter from the Ministry of Home Affairs. It said that the parents of fallen soldiers were being 'compensated'. Families of Kargil war heroes were being allotted a filling station in return for their service to the nation.

Mani says the letter came as a shock. 'I'd just started getting back to a normal life with the help of Prof. Nayyar, Karan and Timmie. And then they came up with something that derailed me from my path of peace and acceptance,' she says. Prof. Nayyar, too, was unhappy about the government's stand on this scheme. Anuj was gone and nothing could make up for this loss, in cash or kind.

Moreover, the family did not want anything they were not prepared to manage or run. But they also did not want to sell off the filling station that the government had given them.

The family chose to ignore the letter and got on with their lives. Mani was back in the library, Karan resumed his studies and Poppin wrote poems for Anuj and managed his consulting firm. As a child, Anuj loved watching his father feed the stray dogs in the neighbourhood. So he started doing it again.

Gurudwara Bangla Sahib offered the Maha Vir Shaheed Captain Anuj Nayyar a sword in honour of his sacrifice and held a prayer meeting for him. Prof. Nayyar received the sword from the gurdwara board. The moment he held the sword, he knew something divine was in it. Standing beside the sarovar, facing the majestic takht that seated the Guru Grant Sahib, he lifted the sword. As he silently closed his eyes to bow to his son, the chanting grew louder in the background: '*Amar rahe ... amar rahe ...* Anuj Nayyar *amar rahe.*'

The sword still resides on the mantlepiece at his home with his father right beside him.

Prof. Nayyar believed in keeping Anuj alive rather than succumbing to his physical absence. He often talked to his son's photos on the wall. 'I know that Anuj was closer to his father than anyone else. In the academy he was either on a call with him or his fiancée. There were times when he'd just block the telephone line for hours,' Col. Paresh says with a laugh.

The issue of the filling station popped up again when Timmie's father visited the Nayyar residence. 'Why do you want to forsake such an honour,' he asked, as the parents sat in silence. Though he tried to reason with the Nayyars, Timmie's father knew they were clear about what they did or did not need to get on with life after Anuj.

'My family doesn't need this simply because we don't believe in pay-outs in exchange for the lives of soldiers,' said Prof. Nayyar. 'There are families of many war heroes and officers who might need this more than us,' he explained.

Timmie's father replied, 'Just to be clear, this filling station is not being provided to you. Instead, it is being provided to Anuj for his ultimate sacrifice. You would only be caretakers of his property.'

This line of thinking seemed to strike a chord with Prof. Nayyar. He could make peace with the offer as it was going to be Anuj's possession of which he was merely a caretaker. The decision was made. Kargil Heights Filling Station was set to be a new chapter in the legacy of Capt. Anuj Nayyar, MVC.

Sunshine Amidst Dark Clouds

Anuj's death had done to Prof. Nayyar what age had not. The loss had slowed him down. He ate less, avoided talking to people and did not share his grief with anyone. 'I never knew sorrow to be scary,' says Karan, 'but his was.'

The filling station brought back the father Karan wanted to see. Prof. Nayyar found a purpose in life. It was like bringing Anuj back – giving birth to him and raising him again.

———

The one that keeps grief from turning into debilitating depression is routine. So the Nayyar family got busy in the day-to-day and followed a set schedule. Prof. Nayyar would leave the house early in the morning. Mani left for the library at 10 a.m. Karan, who was pursuing undergraduate studies at Jamia Hamdard University, would stay back in college till it was time for his parents to return home.

Prof. Nayyar was a hands-on manager at the filling station. He liked to reach early, clean the premises and interact with customers. In an incident often recalled by Indian Oil officials, Prof. Nayyar made a customer clean the floor when he tried to make it off after spitting in the station premises. He had a bucket of water brought in and said, 'It's your soldier's filling station and it can't be disrespected like this.'

In those days, few filling stations had drinking water available. Mani remembers Anuj telling her that soldiers were trained to go without water for long hours, but it upset him that there were few places on the Indian roads where street vendors and rickshaw pullers could find clean drinking water. Prof. Nayyar had a commercial water cooler installed at the station after which it was common to see many locals queue up every day with their cans and bottles.

It had been almost a year since the filling station had been in operation and yet the harassment and frequent confrontations with the government officials continued. It was around then that Prof. Nayyar started to think that extraordinary measures were needed to win this 'war' against constant demands for bribes and red-tape-ism.

On 26 July 2001, Prof. Nayyar was invited by Prime Minister Atal Bihari Vajpayee and Home Minister L.K. Advani to the Ashoka Hotel in Delhi to commemorate the second anniversary of India's victory in Kargil.

Prof. Nayyar decided to attend the event to get an audience with top cabinet ministers and share his harrowing experience of running the filling station. As the speeches and discussions continued, Anuj's father felt dejected with the show of sympathy.

The sacrifice of Kargil martyrs had not ended with the ceasefire. Their families were suffering every day. Elderly parents were being threatened by goons and thugs to sign off the filling stations allotted to them. Widows were still waiting for their pension. But the netas and babus continued to make a mockery of the lives the country had lost in the name of national security.

Prof. Nayyar felt his blood boil. The applause that followed the prime minister's speech seemed to pierce his heart. He knew he had to act fast to get Vajpayee's attention, even at the risk of his own safety. As the prime minister made his way through the audience, Prof. Nayyar rose from his seat. He took a decisive step towards a better future for the families of all Kargil heroes.

The outcome was dramatic. Prof. Nayyar was held back by commandos who searched him for weapons as a reporter from a TV news channel ran towards him for a sound byte. He was, after all, the man who had pushed through two well-built guards to get within Vajpayee's earshot. He addressed the prime minister in a furious tone: 'This Vijay Diwas (victory day) that you're celebrating today has come at the cost of my son. I've also been fighting a war. I also want to celebrate a Vijay Diwas the day I win the battle against your bureaucracy.'

While Vajpayee was led away from the commotion, the home minister stopped to listen to the aggrieved father. He immediately ordered the commandos to stand down and asked Prof. Nayyar to step forward. He offered him a glass of water and asked him to share his grievances. Over the next few minutes, Prof. Nayyar told Advani about the ordeal his family had been through. He told the minister that he did not want any parent to go through this trauma.

In the following weeks, the filling station got a government-approved electricity connection after direct intervention of the Ministry of Home Affairs. The discussion with the home minister also led to an inquiry into the conduct of all those who had harassed the Nayyars and openly asked for bribes.

The family had fought as valiantly as the soldier they had sent to Kargil in 1999. Two years after the victory in the mountains, the family had won their own war.

The Legacy of the Tiger of Drass

Capt. Anuj Nayyar is remembered in many ways. Symbolic and material, his values have been celebrated in the last twenty-one years. The road leading to the Janakpuri house where Anuj grew up was renamed to Shaheed Captain Anuj Nayyar Marg in 2000. The same road now also leads to Shaheed Captain Anuj Nayyar Sarvodaya Bal Vidyalaya, a school which was renamed in his honour. Every year his mother gives scholarships to the toppers of each class.

Army Public School, Dhaula Kuan has kept his memory alive. The school's annual trophies, awarded to the top performers in academics, sports and extracurricular activities, bear Capt. Anuj Nayyar's name. The school also has a heroes' gallery which holds the memorabilia of fallen soldiers in Kargil 1999: Capt. Anuj Nayyar, MVC (1992), 17 Jat; Capt. Sanjiv Dahiya (1991), 5 Rajput; Lt Vijayant Thapar, VrC (1993), 2 Rajasthan Rifles; Lt Amit Verma (1993), 9 Mahar; Maj. Vivek Gupta, MVC (1987), 2 Rajasthan Rifles; Capt. Aditya Mishra (1991), Ladakh Scouts.

His name was memorialized in the school's martyrs' gallery, and the reading hall of South Campus, Delhi University was named after him. The University of Delhi has continued to pay tribute to Capt. Anuj Nayyar in the coming years. Captain Anuj Nayyar Memorial Gold Medal for master's in informatics and communication is awarded to the highest performing students every year.

In 2003, a Bollywood movie called *LOC Kargil*, directed by J.P. Dutta, was released to highlight the stories of Kargil war and the fallen soldiers. Capt. Anuj Nayyar's character was played by Saif Ali Khan in the film. Later that year, Ashwini Chaudhary made the Hindi film *Dhoop*, based on the Nayyar family's struggle to get the filling station up and running. Om Puri played the captain's father in the film.

Infantrymen kept Capt. Anuj Nayyar's stories alive for filmmakers, reporters and civilians through their accounts of the war. Sepoy Tejbir Singh from 17 Jat named his newborn son after Anuj, whom he had served on reconnaissance missions in Kargil. For Brig. Anil Sharma his birthday has become a sombre affair after he lost Anuj on that day in 1999.

Civilians too left no stone unturned in keeping Capt. Anuj Nayyar's story alive for the new generations.

His life and afterlife have given many beautiful relationships to his family and loved ones. Students, biking groups, journalists, artists, filmmakers, army aspirants, civilian groups and individuals have time and again added new dimensions to Anuj's memories.

Rashtriya Riders – a group of bikers on a mission to develop an ethical riding culture and pay homage to the Indian armed forces and fallen soldiers – has been pivotal in bringing Anuj's life to mainstream knowledge.

The Brave Martyr Foundation and its chairman Syed Algazi; the DESH Foundation and its founders Anasuya Mitra and Adrija Sen, along with members Vikas Manhas and Baisakhi; and the Vivekanand Society of Australia have played notable roles in coordinating various memorial ceremonies, interviews and events.

Thousands of followers on social media who continue to contribute time, talk about Anuj and other soldiers like him and encourage others to read about their story are the unsung heroes of this nation.

They are the real reason why the flame of the immortal soldier never dies out.

A poem from a father to his son:

My son, the Tiger of Drass,
You live in our heart,
Your smile is as fresh as ever.

Your saga of valour and fearless determination
Shall be remembered for ever
In the hearts of the Jats and history of the army.

You are a beacon of inspiration.
You taught us how to love and
How to remember.

Remember we will what you gave us,
Remember we will the loss,
The years to be spent together and
The years your brother missed.

Remember we will
The profound grief and pride, and
The history you made
For the coming generations.

Epilogue

Till 2018, the memories of Capt. Anuj Nayyar were a closely guarded possession of his family. His mother had packed away his belongings and refused to look at them for almost twenty years. His boxes were opened only after Himmat Singh Shekhawat and Shivaditay Modi visited the family. They were from a group called Rashtriya Riders, a biking group that was retracing the footsteps of Kargil war heroes in the summer of 2018. By then, they had met the families of Capt. Saurabh Kalia, Capt. Vikram Batra, Maj. Sudhir Walia, Capt. Vijayant Thapar and many others. Anuj's story was inspiring and Himmat, deeply moved by the humility of the Nayyars, wanted to share it with the world. 'I wanted to know more about him. I didn't want to settle for just his letters,' says Himmat.

Himmat and Shivaditay established contact with Karan, who until then was also keeping Anuj's memories to himself.

Himmat's *himmat* (courage/confidence) convinced Mani to walk down the memory lane and relive Anuj's life. She knew everything he was and everything he could have been; but the rest of the world also needed to know. Every nook and every corner of the house told a different story about Anuj. Through endless nights of silent tears, days full of calls with Anuj's friends, coursemates and fellow Kargil warriors, and the experiences of Prof. Nayyar, they pieced together Anuj's life.

Meetings with Anuj's childhood friends, classmates from school and close family members brought out the stories from his personal life. His batchmates from the army were glad to share stories from their days at the NDA, IMA and YOs. Officers and jawans of 17 Jat were also interviewed for crucial details of his profession and life away from family.

But something felt incomplete; there was still a gap between Anuj and his story. The information gathered was not enough to chart his life.

The Nayyars who had not thought of accessing Anuj's personal effects until then were now faced with the interest of a biographer. Mani and Karan knew that things would have been different with Prof. Nayyar around. He understood Anuj in a way that they did not.

After discussions with a few army officials, Himmat and others decided to retrace Anuj's short but eventful life in the mountains of Drass and Mushkoh, where he slept on stone beds, drank from natural springs, pitched tents with fellow warriors and led the assault on the Pimple Complex.

The next step was to find the unit that he was a part of before and during the war. It emerged that they were posted close to the heights where Anuj had left them in 1999. So contacts were harnessed, permissions sought and visits arranged. Karan, Himmat and Shivaditay, along with Vikas Manhas (a patriot who has dedicated his life to serving the families of fallen soldiers) and Rahul

Pathania, were off to a pilgrimage of sorts – through the plains of Pir Panjal via Uri to the Kargil War Memorial and finally the Pimple Complex.

The visit was scheduled for 14–15 August 2018. Despite murmurs of militant tension in the region, the group decided to meet Anuj's mates from 17 Jat, Charlie Company and other units.

Col. Paresh Gupta, Anuj's IMA buddy, was stationed in Srinagar at the time as a training officer for Jammu and Kashmir Light Infantry. Karan says, 'Thanks to Col. Gupta, we came to know that we had barely scratched the surface of Anuj Bhai's time in the armed forces.' Most of his story as a soldier, as an officer and as an individual had its genesis in his years at the NDA and the IMA. Col. Gupta not only made incidents from their academy days come alive, but he also helped the group to find the right course-mates and officers who could fill in the gaps in Anuj's story.

The search for the 'tiger of Drass' led the group to 17 Jat Battalion's Uri base camp.

Meetings with the men of 17 Jat unravelled details of how the war was fought and won by Capt. Anuj Nayyar and other brave men. The sepoys, lance naiks and naiks – who had been promoted to the ranks of naib subedars and subedars – poured their hearts out as they remembered the brave captain's exploits in the mountain peaks of Kargil.

Their voices grew louder as recounted moments of excitement, thrill and challenge. They spoke in hushed tones when they relived setbacks, despair and death.

Subedars Man Singh, Manoj Kumar, Vinod Kumar and about fifteen other Kargil veterans sat in a room as they remembered Anuj. It was more of a celebration than a recounting with a heavy heart.

After the interviews, Karan, Himmat and Shivaditay continued on their journey to the Kargil War Memorial. There, while walking through the memorial stones for the deceased soldiers, Karan wore a T-shirt that once belonged to his brother. Finally, to find the last fragments of Anuj's life, the group proceeded to the Pimple Complex.

The nullah, the mountain trough where the Charlie Company had waited before mounting their attack on the Pimple Complex, was their first stop. The ascent took longer than usual with five civilians. It was getting cold but sunlight peeping through the ridges lent a degree of warmth to the mountain slopes.

Karan was at peace. The journey that would unravel his brother to the world was now truly under way. It was time for him and his mother to air the trunk full of memories and release Anuj from being a captive of the past. For his part, Himmat was happy to see him united with his brother.

In Delhi, Mani had started putting words together for the first pages of the book. It was an emotional walk for her, down the lanes that she had avoided for nineteen summers. She knew who Anuj was. She had shaped him. But she did not know how much he had evolved by himself. That was the story that Karan, Himmat and Shivaditay brought home.

Late-night meetings, poring over war logs, interviews with majors, colonels, brigadiers and generals, discussions at ground zero, and the episode of the Kargil Heights Filling Station led to a book that was surely worthy of the life that Anuj lived.

Anuj's patriotism was his faith. His faith in the idea that he belonged to an integrated nation, his faith in the idea that the nation respected him, his faith in the idea that he could protect it.

He wished to uphold its integrity always. His ideas were held by a belief that there was something worth fighting for in this country.

This story was written to bring a boy's passion for his nation to light. This is the story of Captain Anuj Nayyar, MVC – the Tiger of Drass.

Appendix – Letters Sent Home

Letter 1

Karan, be so hard and tough that, people think twice before troubling you. One should stay away from you after seeing your confidence and your hard body. Tough bodies don't belong to body builders or models, they belong to men.

Letter 2

Page 1

My Dear Mani,

This is to wish you a very happy birthday. You have always been there, whenever I needed your guidance (that is another matter that I never followed it!). It used to be a test for me to fool you into believing the lies that I concocted.

90% of the time you would catch me, but I did get away with 10% of them. The incidents I have told you about my school are only 1% of them. When I joined NDA, my only regret was that you were not in favour. But I was confident that I could prove my worth - my salt. And that is exactly what I am doing. In the future I want, me and my wife to be exactly like you and dad. Only a lady like you control me. Everyone else raised their hands in submission but you still stood solid. Love you.

Your son,
Anuj.

Page 2

Dear Mani,
   You mean the world to me?
"Mom, it's a day for remembering
helpful things you've said
and caring things you've done
and for thanking you for the love
that makes each memory special."
Have a very happy birthday.
I am because of you, my career is because of you, my life is because of you and OUR FAMILY is so strongly bonded only because of your magnetism.
I LOVE YOU.

All my love,
Anuj

Letter 3

Enjoy yourself as I am enjoying myself. Don't worry self, I'm really enjoying myself. Life has become easy and I'm getting 5 to 6 hours of sleep. That is quite sufficient.I am trying to improve on my academics. And like last term, I'll do it this time too. Well, gotta go now.
Write soon, or else…

Love,
Anuj

Letter 4

Mani
Send some eatables. Take care of Karan. Take care of Poppin.

Dad
Complete the book. Progress in your lectures and business. Take care of Karan and Mani. Don't dare fight with Mani. Don't worry about me. This life is not hard at all.

Karan
Keep running. Let your mind control your body.
Never give up on a route. Never walk while on route. Learn new recipes. Be happy. M in me. Learn to ride your bullet. Make new girlfriend.

A quotation for you all:
"Join the army,
Visit new places,

Meet new people…
And kill them."

A soldier never kneels down, except in front of his gun. Never till he is alive.

Love for you 3 only.
Anuj Beta + Bhaiya

Letter 5

My definition:-
Karan - My heart and soul.
Dad - My best and closest friend.
Mani - My everything.
My heart and soul and best friend should keep my everything happy.

Letter 6

Once more telling you the same thing, don't trouble Mani and Poppin too much. They are working hard for us. Let them enjoy themselves till I come back. After that, I'll take over.

Letter 7

My dear Karan.

I have come to know about your marks. They are not as good as I expected. You will not be able to form a strong base for IX and above doing this way. In order to pass entrance exam, one must have good IQ. For good IQ, you must work hard in the junior classes. If you work hard now, you will enjoy as I did.

If you work hard now and enjoy in XI or XII, even then you will be able to do better than me. I passed 4 exams out of 4 attempted. 100% result, you can be better than me.

If you can be better than me then why not do it and enjoy a little later. If you are better than me then it means that you can get better opportunity than even NDA. SO BETTER WORK HARD NOW.

Letter 8

Dearest Mom, Dad and Karan.

Yaa Hoo!!

I have got conjunctivitis (Thank you God!!). You must be shocked at my fun but well, that is the way an illness is celebrated in the academy. It sure is a welcome change. Just imagine, bed rest for 2 days. Just fabulous. I sure am lucky!!

Letter 9

These sure are many reasons because which I'm always thinking about you 3.

I love you 3.

I adore you 3.

I miss you 3.

I care for you 3.

I think of you 3.

I like 3 of you.

I worry for you 3.
I want to meet you 3.
I'd love to see you 3.
Take care and so will I.

Love Ya,
Anuj

Letter 10

Page 1

Dear Mom and Dad.

This is my 2nd letter to you all today. I had run you up today and on doing so, I came to know that dad had scolded Karan for 1 hour. For just losing a piddly tape recorder.
I don't care about the value of the item lost/destroyed but take this as my 1st and last warning. No one will scold Karan for anything. No bloody item is as precious as my Brother's smiling face. I did not like it when Karan told me that …

Page 2

… Dad had scolded him. Under no circumstances will anyone scold or trouble Karan in my absence.

Let this be the last time I am hearing such a complaint from my dearest, sweetest most INNOCENT brother who does not know even how to make MISTAKES.

One hour is a far prospect, Karan - my naughtiest brother is not to be scolded for even a single minute, no matter how big a mistake he commits.

Rest all is fine here. I am enjoying myself and missing you three chaps a lot. Take care of my Kannu.

Love you.

Love you all sooooo much.

Anuj

Letter 11

I suppose I haven't mentioned my very first PUNISHMENT. Well, I had Drill in the morning and the metal sole of my drill boot came off. The drill instructors awarded me 2 endurance treks. I was really overjoyed to find 5 of us in the same boat. In Endurance Trek (E.T.), we have to wear dungarees, our Defence Military Shows and on top of that our commando/tracking pouch (small bags hung on shoulders, and with the weight belt). This whole equipment weighs about 18 kgs. Now, we have to run a distance of about 6-7 kms of hilly terrain in 35 minutes. I really enjoyed both of my treks.

Another one of my adventures was the BO (Bajri Order) in which the same packs are filled with 'Bajri', and the weight is over 40 kgs. It's really good for your back!!

Penning down for now, will write more astonishing facts next time!!!

Love you and missing you a lot especially nowadays.

Your forever,

Anuj.

Letter 12

Dearest Dad,

You are the best choice of a dad for me. You are ideal stuff. By the way, you must be having a question at the back of your mind that – why is Anuj taking on all the tough activities. Well, if you don't have that question then Mom must be having it. Well, the answer is that many cadets come and go without taking the challenges that I have taken up. Well, they just survive through NDA, but Dad - I am your son and I am not just going to survive. I am going to LIVE through this experience. I am not a coward who is dragging himself through this phase of life. I am going to walk out with pride and self-satisfaction and for that I have to accomplish the most challenging of tasks.

Have to go now.

Write to you as soon as I get your letter. Love You

Yours exclusively
Anuj Nayyar

Letter 13

Page 1

One more thing, whenever we get a letter, the 1st termers who has for the letter has to do 60 push ups to take the letter (a tradition amongst us). So, if you want me to build up my body then write as many letters you can.

Page 2

This is the IDEAL LIFE. If I had taken up anything else it would have been my life's biggest and most fatal mistake.

Letter 14

Physically, I may be 1600 kms from you 3, but you 3 know that I am still there in BE – 187, in your heart, and so are all of you (Mom, Dad and my Karan). Be strong and lend me your strength.

Letter 15

Dad,
   You are very important to all 3 of us, get well immediately.

Mom,
Take care of Dad and Karan के कान खींच कर रखो, नहीं तो बिगड़ जाएगा।

Karan,
Beta, enjoy yourself, but keep in mind your responsibilities in my absence and also your studies.

I love you all.
(The best family that I can ever have!)

Letter 16

Page 1

Dearest Mom,
   I wish I was there with you on your and Dad's Birthday.
I Love You.
   You are the "BEST" Mom in the world.
   WE LOVE YOU ALOT

From Your Kids
Anuj
Karan & Timmie

Page 2

Have a great day and miss me too!!
   Your B'day present on the day I get commissioned (So, choose your watch).
   You're the best Mom I could ever have had.
   Stop worrying about your son going to the Army. He's meant for it.
   Those two buggers will never know your (real) value because they've never stayed away from you like I have.

Letter 17

After God made earth, he made man. To bridge the gap between himself and men, he made Mothers. So, I love you.

Enjoy yourself. I don't know what would have happened if someone else was my mother. She would have landed up in the asylum by now. You sure are tough!!

Keep up the good work and the courage. Another star is coming up.

Lots of love,
Your loving son, Anuj.

Letter 18
13 June 1999

Dad, that situation has yet to arrive which your son cannot face like a Nayyar!!
No fear ... ever!!

Letter19
22 June 1999

Dear dad,

Got your inspiring letter at 14th June. Don't worry, I've yet to face an opponent who can win from me. That day can never come when I have to admit defeat. Fear was never in the dictionary you gave me as my dad. Well, you are 200% right, The ground and air never hide anything. I have honed up my skills in the art of fighting with weapon, knives and bare hands too. Don't worry because nothing ever worries your son. Just worried about you 5 (Mom, you, Kannu, Timmie & Naughty). Take care of yourself and my gentleman officer's promise we'll celebrate your 25th anniversary in August.

Dad, take care of Mani. I know she worries a lot. You too must be getting solid kick for letting me join the army. Worry not. Your son is on your side always although, I can't take your side openly against Mom. Bhai she's head of our family na!!

Gotta go. Take care and keep smiling, it always makes me smile.

Love,
Anuj.

Letter 20
29 June 1999

Dad,
You taught me never to be afraid. And it's only because of you that I'm fearless. It's because of you my men are proud of my courage. It's because of you that my men have blind faith in me. Dad, I'm become what I am because I have a friend in my father. I'll always keep your head high and you'll always be proud of me. That's a promise from you son. Luv You. Anuj

Letter 21
30 June 1999

Hi Tiger,

Got your letter and came to know about your Shimla trip. Good, keep it up, Bhai. I'm proud of you. Are you doing something about Ludhiana? C'mon.

Sorry about the handwriting, there's no light. Writing by moonlight!!

Don't worry about me. Just be proud of me. Then when I come over I'll tell you all the experiences and you can boast about your bhai.

Anyway, you enjoy yourself and keep smiling. You and your Bhabhi must take care of everybody. I'm relying on you two.

Kaddu? Well, to tell you a secret, she calls me also by that name. So don't worry. Bada Kaddu and Chota Kaddu … Bhai-Bhai! No hassles.

Gotta go now. Love you.
Your Bhai,
Anuj Bhai.

Letter 22

"The solution to the problem lies within an area with no problem."

Testimonials

I MET ANUJ IN the summer of 1993 at the entrance gate of Echo Squadron in the NDA. The first meeting was strange as we came from two different backgrounds – he a civilian and I an army kid. Yet our personalities seemed to match. Little did we know that our destinies would be intertwined for the next four years: three in the NDA and one in the IMA. I share great memories with Anuj, but some need special mention. What seemed to be mere instances at the time were actually building blocks in the development of his character. We were sports buddies. When other cadets would venture out to Pune town on Sundays, Anuj and I would follow our own regime. After breakfast, we would play volleyball for two hours without break, followed by a thousand crunches and a packet of Marlboro cigarettes. While Anuj was good at volleyball, my forte was crunches. But he would never give up and we would religiously complete the target for the exercise. Little did I know that he was following his creed of 'never give up'.

At the IMA, he had sneaked in a Bullet 500-cc motorcycle in our final term. Being in the same company – Naushera – we again continued with our sports regime on Sundays, followed by a session of beer, which was officially allowed now. For Saturday evenings we had a different plan. Late in the evening we would take off on the motorcycle for a long ride. No destination in mind, we would just drive for an hour, halt for tea and cigarettes and get back to the academy. Anuj had a mind of his own; being straigtjacketed was not him. The individuality, which is a hallmark of an outstanding leader and a soldier, was visible in his acts from the very beginning.

Wars and warriors are remembered through timelines and events. Capt. Anuj Nayyar, son of Satish and Meena Nayyar, walked tall in the battlefield, humbling adversaries on the icy peaks of Kargil in Operation Vijay, in 1999. He was a fierce, soldier, an officer and leader par excellence and an eternal friend. Hail Anuj, who fought valiantly 'for the ashes of his fathers and the temples of his gods'.

Col. Ashok Kumar Thakur

Serious Yet Fun-Loving, Mature Yet Footloose

Life is special, filled with memorable moments, and yet it can be hard at times. One such period that had a deep impact on my life were my days at the NDA with my dear friend Capt. Anuj Nayyar, MVC. The NDA brings together many a band of brothers from across India. In 1993, I developed a bond with a young gun from Delhi who was a blend of many traits – serious yet fun-loving, mature yet footloose, passionate yet balanced, loving and caring yet with killer instincts – a boy one would love to hate for being near perfect. Though our sqaudrons were different, the rigorous training and the commotion in our life kept us bonded through the various activities on campus. However, it was in the IMA that Anuj and I grew closer. He always acted tough but was just as soft, and it was his love for someone special that made him open up to me. Like any other boy of his age, he had taken his love for the girl to a new level. He lost track of time while talking to her on the landline, which was in my room for official purposes. The facility of outgoing calls was restricted to local numbers only but the same was not true for incoming calls, of which Anuj took advantage. I found him glued to the phone whenever he got time off from training. I wondered who this lucky girl was and he promised to introduce her to me on his day of commissioning. I discovered his brotherly side when Karan landed up at the academy. I was shocked when Anuj said that he planned on keeping his brother in his room for a night. This was against the rules but I, despite being one of the custodians of discipline, turned a blind eye to it. The consequences could have been dire but then we were trained to deal with danger; so the one-night stay got extended to more nights and Anuj took great risks to make his brother attend all his favourite events such as boxing and volleyball matches.

True to his word, Anuj introduced me to his fiancée on the day he got the pips on his shoulders. Time flew by and we met again in Mhow during the Young Officers' course and shared accommodation in the same complex. He had matured in his conduct, and carried himself like someone who had taken full charge of his life. Our conversation was now more about professional preparedness unlike earlier. He would speak more of his father and his bond with him as a friend. I witnessed this father–son affection when his father sent him his favourite bike from Delhi. My relation with Anuj had by now grown deeper and intimate – just one look and we knew what the other was thinking. We parted ways after completing a commando course at Belgaum with the understanding that I would attend his wedding, but with a warning that I should not expect his time nor his attention when he was with his girl.

Few months later, the news of him laying down his life in Kargil for the nation came as a blow. Unable to accept the truth, I called up the girl he was to marry. I was shaking and in tears and was consoled by her. I had lost a dear friend but his memories are still fresh after almost two decades. Rest in peace, my dear friend. The band of brothers still shares a strong bond just because of your faith in us. One for all and all for one.

Col. Paresh Gupta

A Trustworthy Friend

I got inducted to the roadhead camp called 80R early morning of 8 July 1999. I knew that 17 Jat had gone in for an attack the previous night. The outcome of the assault was not known yet but I just hoped to catch up with Anuj when he came down and exchange old memories, laugh and gain first-hand knowledge of the situation and understand what needed to be done. I went and sat on the narrow track awaiting his return, or some news.

Battle-worn soldiers were returning, some were forming part of the administrative echelons responsible for pushing up ammunition and supplies. A fair number of injured soldiers were being brought back. I had been in Kashmir for two years at the time and had seen many such scenes, not on the same scale though. Somehow as the injured soldiers passed by, the hope of seeing Anuj started to fade. Finally, I spotted a few tall, strong and hardy-looking soldiers who seemed to be from the Jats, I thought. I stopped one guy and asked, '*Nayyar sahab kahan hain?*' '*Sahab* attack *mein gaye the, shahid ho gaye,*' he said. His tears and trembling voice left no doubt about the authenticity of his statement. I got up without a word and started walking back with the soldiers. I did not cry for the first few minutes but as the reality of not seeing a good friend again dawned upon me, the tears began to spill over. I cried as I walked back to the camp with the Jats for next twenty minutes or so. No one asked me the reason, everyone had lost something that night and, in some manner, everyone was mourning. To this date my eyes moisten when I think about that day. Anuj and I had not known each other for long except when we landed up in the same company and platoon at the IMA. He was a bull as far as physical fitness was concerned and I admired him for that. Be it tactical camp or cross-country practice, if anyone needed help and asked Anuj for it, he was there with the person till the end. This attitude was not restricted to his days at the academy. During the YOs, Anuj kept his motorcycle hidden in a part of the Infantry School. If I ever needed a bike to go out, it was always his, knowing fully well that if caught, we both could have been sent back to our units. He was a large-hearted, trustworthy friend and I will remember him that way.

Col. Sarvinder Singh

A True Team Man

This episode is about the privilege of experiencing Anuj's friendship. We were in the fourth term when I injured my knee while playing basketball. The ligaments of my right knee were torn and I was transferred to the military hospital in Pune for a longish time.

I was discharged near the term end. I needed to pass academics and physical training to move to the next semester. I cleared the written exam without much trouble. I also cleared the physical tests involving upper body strength. I feared the running test the most because of the injury.

One late evening, I was in my room and mulling over my options, maybe even the loss of a term. Just then Anuj came by and we started discussing how to address the problem. He left the room saying that we will meet the next day at the starting line of the race track. I reached the track and found Anuj and Ashok already there. I assumed they were there to motivate me. They had bunked their classes for this.

The run commenced. I was barely able to drag my legs. The PT instructors moved alongside us on bicycles. I was trailing behind when Anuj and Ashok lifted me from both sides. I was airborne; I was flying! In no time I had crossed the halfway mark. The instructors threatened Anuj with dire consequences and punishment. But he was undeterred. We managed to complete the run but finished a minute late.

After much deliberation, the PT instructors declared the result. They cleared me, overwhelmed by the display of team spirit. The senior instructor later asked Anuj, jokingly, 'Are you at war? We see such spirit only during war.' Well, that was Anuj in the making.

Cdr Ankur Kulshrestha

Anuj, the Strategist

I remember Anuj as a person with immense mental strength. However tense or difficult the situation, Anuj was calm, composed and had faith in himself that he would come out of it. And this strength of his diffused to all those around him. Like a true leader, his face and body language would exude confidence, motivating others to believe in him. Behind that was an uncanny mind quickly analysing situations and arriving at the best course of action. No wonder Anuj led his team to one of the most famous victories in Indian military history. In his martyrdom the nation gained a hero and I lost an ever-smiling and compassionate friend.

There are many qualities and achievements for which Anuj is remembered. Not touching on those, I will recount a volleyball game from September 1995 at the NDA, where Anuj's mental power won the day for Echo Squadron. Team Echo did not have a formidable line-up – I was the booster, we had a rookie spiker (both play at the net) and all over the court was Anuj. He had one of the speediest underhands I have seen, with an ability to receive the ball anywhere behind the attack line and place it anywhere in his own or opponent's court. Anuj realized that with a weak team, the only way to win was by messing with the opponent's head. He put both his mind and speedy underhand to good use. What followed was selective sledging, deceiving calls and precise placement of the ball in our opponent's court. This sowed the seeds of deep confusion in their team, which resulted in infighting. The rest of us joined in as actors in the play being directed by Anuj from the centre of the court. Anuj did his best to add fuel to the infighting, and soon Echo Squadron, clearly the weaker team at play, found the confidence to outsmart a formidable opponent. Strategizing a game won the day for our team in September 1995. The same tactics saved the day for the nation on July 7 1999.

Col. Shyam Kumar

The Man to Follow

The National Defence Academy Khadakwasla is a premier institution of the Indian defence forces and is called the cradle of leadership, where young impressionable boys are transformed into commanders. Among these young boys, a few always stand out for their maturity, clarity and leadership qualities. Capt. Anuj Nayyar, MVC, was one such cadet who joined the academy in the spring term 1993. It has been my honour to be his squadron-mate and course-mate. I am fortunate to have spent time with this legend and to call him a friend. The spark in Anuj could be seen from his early days when most of us were getting used to the tough academy routine. Never the one to give up, he taught us to keep smiling under the worst of circumstances. He was a friend who would come to your help without thinking twice. I can well imagine that a person who inspired his peers would have been loved by his troops. He epitomized what a soldier should be as he went down fighting at the young age of twenty-three years. It is because of brave sons like him that our flag flutters proudly.

Col. K.S. Thakur

My Comrade

My first meeting with Anuj was at the ground-floor lobby of Echo Squadron at the NDA. It was also the first day of my reporting. We instantly connected over the fact that we both were from Delhi. Over the next three years, all twenty-eight of us from the ninetieth batch of Echo Squadron built and shared a strong bond. Anuj was always seen as the dedicated, balanced and promising cadet who never hesitated to help anyone in need. His zeal towards the team, to be involved in critical decisions about the day-to-day functioning of the squadron, showed. Having proved his mettle in the field in sports, especially boxing and cross-country runs, academics and physically exhaustive outdoor camps, Anuj was a role model to many of us. It is a matter of great pride for us that the world knows him as one of the heroes of the Kargil war. Salute, comrade.

Col. Rohit Yadav

Cheerful Comrade

Anuj had a positive energy and I could feel it every time I was around him. I remember him being cheerful even in the most challenging times. His immense *josh*, course spirit and camaraderie were three of the many great qualities that defined him as one of the finest. He was the person I would go for advice or assistance. The news of his martyrdom was devastating; he deserved to live a hundred years.

Wg Cdr Sharad Gaur

Determined Anuj

Anuj was dear to all of us in Echo Squadron. Not only to his classmates, but to his seniors and juniors as well. This was due to the matured and determined outlook he had developed as well as his pleasant and helpful nature. Extremely hardworking, Anuj was an inspiration to many of us during our NDA, IMA and YO days and will remain so in the times to come.

Col. Salil M.P.

Salute, Dearest Brother

The Anuj I remember was extremely dedicated and organized. He had a plan for every situation; the deficiencies he made up with his dedication. What a fine general he would have made if not for that tryst with destiny. But then such is warfare. Dedication to the cause was perhaps hardwired into him. That he was meant for soldiering was evident in the various camps at NDA. The real-life Rambo was a one-man army even back then, from navigating to helping stragglers. At one such camp, hungry, thirsty and lost in the wilderness, the squadron mates had all but given up when, in true Rambo style, Anuj picked up the LMG and took off. The rest of us had no choice but to follow him and soon enough we found the next checkpoint!

Col. Salil Kumar

The Kargil Heroes of 17 Jat

3169696Y Havildar Kumar Singh, VrC (P)

Havildar Kumar Singh of Charlie Company, 17 Jat served the battalion for twenty-one years. In the battle of Pimple 2 (Kargil, 1999) he led a section from the front, lobbying grenades and mounting direct assaults over enemy bunkers. He was among the men that joined the operation at the Pimple Complex with Capt. Anuj Nayyar. In the assault on Pimple 2, he killed three enemy troops and captured two enemy bunkers. This valiant effort cost him his life but his supreme sacrifice led to capture of the peak.

3169828F Havildar Hari Om, SM (P)

Havildar Hari Om of Charlie Company, 17 Jat served in this battalion for twenty-one years. In the battle of Pimple 2, he led a section to the front, breaking the section guarded defence of the enemy. His fearless actions and hand-to-hand combat with the enemy motivated others to follow suit. His ascent culminated in the supreme sacrifice but not before clearing two enemy bunkers and killing five enemy troops.

3170559M Havildar Mahavir Singh, SM (P)

Havildar Mahavir Singh of Bravo Company, 17 Jat had served in this battalion twenty 20 years. In the battle of Pimple 2, he led a section of troops across the enemy flank. On reaching his objective, he cleared one enemy bunker, killed two enemy troops and recovered two enemy weapons. While advancing towards the objective, he got injured and succumbed to his injuries.

3172785H Naik Balwan Singh, SM (P)

Naik Balwan Singh led a set of jawans in the assault on Pimple 2 and cleared an enemy bunker by lobbing grenades and ultimately charging directly towards it. Despite being injured by machine gun fire, he kept advancing till the bunker was finally captured. He went on to defend the secured position through the enemy counter-attack before succumbing to injuries on the field.

3188347K Sepoy Surender, SM (P)

Sepoy Surender of Charlie Company, 17 Jat had served in this battalion for our years and three months. In the battle of Pimple 2, he was the Capt. Anuj Nayyar's runner. He shadowed Anuj's campaign through all the heavy enemy artillery, mortar shelling and small arms fire. He remained with him all the way, lobbying grenades and charging at bunkers to his captain's orders. With Anuj, he cleared two enemy bunkers but was critically injured by a grenade which led to his death.

3188797F Sepoy Puna Ram, SM

Sepoy Puna Ram of Delta Company, 17 Jat was the leading scout during the attack on Whaleback. Despite being shot by automatic rifle, he destroyed an enemy bunker which assisted company advance and successful capture of the peak. He was awarded the Sena Medal on 15 August 1999 for his contribution to Operation Vijay.

JC-183456K Subedar Harphool Singh, MiD (P)

Subedar Harphool Singh of Bravo Company, 17 Jat had served in this battalion for twenty-seven years. As the platoon commander of 4 Platoon 4, he along with his unit was assigned the task of capturing Point 4540, followed by Rocky Knob. Despite heavy shelling and automatic fire from enemy bunkers, Subedar Harphool Singh showed exemplary courage and determination in the assault campaign on Point 4540. However, he was fatally wounded while approaching Rocky Knob, and in the process of capturing an enemy bunker. He made the supreme sacrifice in true traditions of the regiment.

JC-488102K Subedar Om Parkash, MiD

Subedar Om Parkash was tasked to carry out pre-emptive commando action to occupy an advance position of enemy in the Pimple Complex. During a stealth operation, Subedar Om Parkash led his commandoes from the front and in a daring and bold action occupied 'thumb' and 'hump' in the mountain complex. He killed two enemy troops and also occupied a 'listening post' which facilitated the capture of Pimple 1.

3168723L Havildar Bhagwan Singh, MiD (P)

Havildar Bhagwan Singh of Charlie Company, 17 Jat, had served in this battalion for twenty-one years and eleven months. In the battle of Pimple 2, he led his section from the front and despite heavy odds motivated his team to continue advancing. He captured two enemy bunkers, killed three enemy troops and recovered three weapons which ultimately led to the successful capture of the peak.

3177220F Naik Rishipal Singh, MiD (P)

Naik Rishipal Singh of Charlie Company, 17 Jat had served in this battalion for sixteen years and two months. In the battle of Pimple 2, he took charge of the section upon the loss of his company commander. He led his section towards capturing enemy bunkers, while killing two enemy troops and recovering two enemy weapons before making the supreme sacrifice.

3180612A Lance Naik Rajesh, MiD (P)

Lance Naik Rajesh of Charlie Company, 17 Jat had served in this battalion for twelve years and four months. In the battle of Pimple 2, he cleared the obstructions for his fellow men by destroying an enemy automatic rifle bunker and killing three Pakistani troops. He fired six rounds of rocket launcher (air burst) to repel the enemy counterattack before getting hit by enemy fire.

3180868H Lance Naik Ramvir Singh

No 3180868H Lance Naik Ramvir Singh had served in this battalion for over twelve years. He was a fighting porter who was carrying medium machine gun ammunition for the Delta Company. He was hit by a splinter, just short of completing his supply run. However, he managed supplied the ammunition which was required to push the enemy counterattack. His injuries from the splinter proved fatal by the end of the attack.

3182134A Lance Naik Vijay Singh, MiD (P)

No 3182134A Lance Naik Vijay Singh had served in this battalion for eleven years and six months. He was undertaking the duties of a fighting porter and carrying medium machine gun ammunition for Delta Company. Just short of his destination during a the Delta Company operation, he was hit by a splinter leading to critical injuries. Despite being injured, he completed his ammunition supply run which helped maintain the company's advantage over enemy counterattack. He later succumbed to his injuries during the operation.

3182641N Lance Naik Rajendra Singh

Lance Naik Rajendra Singh of Bravo Company, 17 Jat had served in this battalion for eleven years. In the battle of Pimple 2, as a part of the two-inch mortar detachment, he provided accurate and effective covering fire to the forward assault units. Undaunted by heavy enemy artillery, mortars and small arms fire, he provided fire support, causing heavy casualties to enemy troops. He continued to repel the counterattack before succumbing to his injuries.

3184853K Sepoy Syodana Ram

Sepoy Syodana Ram had served in this battalion for eight years and three months. He was a fighting porter and was carrying rocket launcher ammunition for the Charlie Company of 17 Jat. While moving to the objective, he was hit by an enemy artillery shell. Despite critical injuries he supplied ammunition required for the capture of Pimple 2.

3185510N Sepoy Dharambir Singh, MiD (P)

Sepoy Dharambir Singh of Charlie Company, 17 Jat had served in this battalion for seven years five months. In the battle of Pimple 2, he was the leading scout for his platoon. Despite heavy enemy artillery, mortar shelling and small arms fire, he showed exemplary courage in crawling up to the enemy bunker and neutralizing it. He lobbed two grenades

inside and killed all the occupants. In his continued advance, he got hit by enemy RPG round and succumbed to his injuries. His sacrifice finally led to the capture of Pimple 2.

3187320A Sepoy Ranveer Singh, MiD (P)

Sepoy Ranveer Singh of Bravo Company, 17 Jat had served in this battalion for four years and eight, 8 months. In the battle of Bimbat, he was the radio operator and runner for Subedar Harphool Singh. While advancing towards enemy bunkers, he saw his platoon commander get hit by an MMG burst. Forsaking his own safety, he crossed the unending enemy fire to reach his platoon commander and help him contact the company commander. All this while, he was simultaneously engaging enemy bunkers with his personal weapon. During his courageous and fearless display of the 17 Jat spirit, he was hit by an enemy sniper leading to his fall.

3187386W Sepoy Vijay Pal, MiD (P)

Sepoy Vijay Pal had served in the battalion for four years and eight months. On 10 June 1999, Sepoy Vijay Pal, radio operator for the Charlie Company, left for a reconnaissance mission to forward posts with his company commander, Capt. Anuj Nayyar. On discovering enemy movement, he assisted Capt. Anuj Nayyar with relaying developments to senior officers and maintain positions to gather more intel. Under heavy automatic fire and shelling, Sepoy Vijay Pal was severely injured. He continued to assist the company commander's radio communication till he finally succumbed to his injuries.

3187414X Sepoy Vinod Kumar, MiD (P)

Sepoy Vinod Kumar of Bravo Company, 17 Jat had served in this battalion for four years. In the battle of Bimbat, he was a member of the rocket launcher detachment. As the company inched towards Rocky Knob, Sepoy Vinod destroyed many enemy bunkers, fighting under constant shelling and automatic fire. During the final push for Rocky Knob, he continuously engaged with the enemy despite being hit by automatic fire till he finally succumbed to his injuries.

3188230L Sepoy Satbir Singh, MiD (P)

Sepoy Satyvir Singh of Charlie Company, 17 Jat had served in this battalion for four years four months. In the battle of Pimple 2, he was a leading scout for the company. During the final assault, he crawled up to the enemy bunker, lobbed two grenades inside and then charged at the bunker, killing two enemy troops and recovering one weapon before getting killed in action.

3188529X Sepoy Anil Kumar

Sepoy Anil Kumar of Bravo Company, 17 Jat had served in this battalion for four years. He was the radio operator and runner for his platoon commander. Not caring for his personal safety, he kept advancing towards the objective for a close combat with the enemy. He displayed exemplary courage in helping his platoon commander till his final last moment.

3188794N Sepoy Hawa Singh, MiD (P)

Sepoy Hawa Singh of Bravo Company, 17 Jat had served in this battalion for three years and eight months. In the battle of Pimple 2, he was the leading scout for his platoon. Despite heavy enemy artillery, Mortar shelling and small arms fire, he kept advancing in front of his platoon, simultaneously engaging the enemy with his weapon. He helped his

platoon commander locate an enemy bunker and lobbed grenades to clear it, followed by a physical assault which led to its successful capture. Later during the ascent to the next bunker, he succumbed to his critical injuries.

3188970A Sepoy Jitendra Singh

Sepoy Jitendra Singh of Bravo Company, 17 Jat had served in this battalion for three years. In the battle of Pimple 2, he was a part of the medium machine gun detachment. Despite being hit by enemy sniper and machine gun fire repeatedly, without caring for his own safety, he continued to provide effective fire support. In the end, the splinter injuries on his face led to his death.

3189068L Sepoy Shish Ram

Sepoy Shish Ram had served in this battalion for three years and six months. He was conducting the duties of fighting porter and evacuating casualties of the Charlie Company when he was hit by an enemy artillery shell. Despite getting critically injured, he continued evacuating the casualties till he succumbed to his injuries.

3189532K Sepoy Gajpal Singh, MiD (P)

Sepoy Gajpal Singh of Bravo Company, 17 Jat had served in this battalion for two years and nine months. In the battle of Bimbat, Sepoy Singh was tasked to mount Rocky Knob with the company. Under heavy enemy automatic fire and shelling, he continued a steady advance towards the enemy bunkers. Despite being injured by enemy fire, Sepoy Gajpal Singh killed two enemy soldiers in a hand-to-hand combat before succumbing to his injuries.

3189697H Sepoy Naresh Kumar

Sepoy Naresh Kumar of Charlie Company, 17 Jat had served in this battalion for three years and two months. In the battle of Pimple 2, he along with his section commander lobbed grenades and killed two enemy troops in close bayonet fighting before being hit by enemy automatic fire and enemy splinter.

3190075N Sepoy Dharambeer Singh, MiD (P)

Sepoy Dharambeer Singh of Bravo Company, 17 Jat had served in this battalion for two years and five months. In the battle of Bimbat, he was part of Platoon 4 which was tasked to climb Rocky Knob after the capture of Point 4540. While advancing under heavy automatic fire and enemy shelling, Sepoy Dharambeer Singh crawled towards an enemy post for a stealth manoeuvre when five automatic rifles opened fire at him. Despite grave injuries, he kept engaging enemy till he was hit with an the RPG which led to his death.

3190727F Sepoy Krishan Kumar, MiD (P)

Sepoy Krishan Kumar of Bravo Company, 17 Jat had served in this battalion for one year and nine months. In the battle of Bimbat he was the leading scout for Platoon 4. Following the capture of Point 4540, he was tasked to scale the heights of Rocky Knob. On reaching the objective, under heavy enemy automatic and artillery fire, he located the enemy bunker for the platoon commander. This led to a successful rocket-launcher assault on the bunker. However, by then he was already critically injured. He kept offering 'covering fire' to the jawans and even resumed the advance when he was hit by another MMG burst resulting in his sacrifice.

JC-488022M Subedar Darshan Singh, COAS Commendation Card

Subedar Darshan Singh led his platoon from the front despite the constant and heavy enemy artillery, automatic and mortar fire. He helped clear two enemy bunkers, killed four enemy troops and captured six weapons. His brave and courageous action led to successful capture of Pimple 2.

JC-488262K Subedar Gurdayal Singh, GOC-in-C Commendation Card

Subedar Gurdayal Singh led from the front under heavy enemy artillery, mortar shelling and automatic fire. He helped capture two enemy bunkers, killed four enemy troops and recovered four weapons while carrying out the assigned mission.

3175223W Havildar Harpal, GOC-in-C Commendation Card

Havildar Harpal was the commander of leading section (Bravo Company) tasked to Point 4540 and capture Rocky Knob. Under heavy enemy automatic fire, which resulted in a gunshot injury, he bravely led his men towards successfully neutralizing a bunker and then the assigned objective.

JC-211099L Subedar Desh Ram, GOC-in-C Commendation Card

Subedar Desh Ram, platoon commander, Bravo Company was tasked to capture Point 4540. Under heavy automatic and artillery fire he led his men from the front, deploying platoon support weapons and destroying the enemy's UMG. He strategically deployed his section from different directions and captured the designated objective for his platoon.

The 17 Jat was awarded the Chief of Army Staff's unit citation on 15 January 2000 for its outstanding performance during Operation Vijay. In addition, the unit was awarded forty-one bravery awards under the following categories. Capt. Anuj Nayyar was awarded the highest gallantry award in the 226-year history of the Jat Regiment.

(a) MVC   - 01
(b) VrC   - 04
(c) SM   - 06
(d) Mention-in-Despatches   - 20
(e) COAS/GOC-in-C Northern Command
     Commendation Cards   - 10

Index

Acknowledgements

This book would not have been possible without the support and guidance of many.

We owe an enormous debt of gratitude to those who gave us constructive criticism on every aspect of book, including Brig. U.S. Bawa, VrC; Brig. Anil Sharma; Col. Deepak Rampal, VrC; Col. Santosh; Col. Shashi Bhushan Ghildiyal, VrC; Col. Ashok Thakur; Col. Paresh Gupta; Col. Chitrasen and Col. Sarvinder Singh. We also thank Gen. V.P. Malik, Lt Gen. Syed Ata Hasnain, Lt Gen. S.K. Saini, Lt Gen. Mohinder Puri and Vishnu Som, who gave their precious time to review portions of the book and shared their commentaries from the war. We are also grateful to the Col. Tapan Singh, Maj. Ravindra Kumar and Capt. Siddharth Thakur for helping with the research that formed the crux of the book, Sub. Man Singh and Sub. Vinod Kumar who fought alongside Capt. Anuj Nayyar in the Charlie Company, and Hav. Sombir.

A shout-out to Vikas Manhas and Rahul Pathania who accompanied us on the Kashmir–Ladakh tour and helped with

Acknowledgements

research. We would also like to thank Anuj's schoolmates from Army Public School, Dhaula Kuan, librarian Dr Tariq Ashraf and the staff of South Campus library. And Harneet Nayyar for painstakingly reading the manuscript and following up with valuable suggestions.

A big thank you to important team members of Rashtriya Riders: Vibhas Bhatnagar, Maj. (R) Ashutosh Garg, Dharmendra Choudhary, Ashwani Bajpai, Amit Poonia, Padam Shekhawat, Mahendra Singh Bhati, Jai Singh Khichi, Ravindra Jangir, Sandeep Sheoran, Mukesh Kothari, Babu Ganesh, Mohit Kothari, Ganesh Saini, Laxmikant Sharma, Ravi Yadav, Rajendra Singh Bhati, Hemant Prajapat, Sanjay Singh Shekhawat, Yatin Arora, Ankit Panday, Ronit Yadav, Karan Singh Rathore, Aayush Agarwal, Riddhi Kapoor, Rohit Singh Rathore and Ranjeet Singh Rathore.

Most importantly, we would like to acknowledge Prof. S.K. Nayyar who left behind an archive of his son's life in the form of letters, photographs and newspaper clippings.

To convert a collection of facts and anecdotes into a comprehensive account is not an easy task. Ankur Gupta, whom we met in December 2018, played an important role here. We are grateful for his help.

We would like to thank Amit Sharma, Krishan Chopra and Suchismita Ukil from HarperCollins for making this book possible.

Sharique Khan, Karan's batch mate from college, introduced the Nayyars to the HarperCollins team deserves a special mention.

Lastly, we would like to thank the Nayyar and Dhingra clan for standing by Anuj's family when they most needed it.

A sincere thanks to anyone we may have missed listing here. We owe so much to anyone who has been with us on this journey.

Special Thanks

The authors would like to thank **Karan Nayyar**, brother of Capt. Anuj Nayyar (MVC), for his help and guidance at every step of conceptualizing, writing and publishing this book.

No journey can be made without a best friend by your side. **Shivaditay Modi** was that friend to Himmat Singh Shekhawat and the team of *The Tiger of Drass*. We thank him for his help on anything that the book demanded.

About the Authors

Meena Nayyar is the mother Capt. Anuj Nayyar, MVC – a retired librarian of Delhi University, a protective mother and a loving wife. For almost two decades, she had locked Anuj away in her memories. The pain of losing her son was too much to talk about, let alone write a book. It was only after she met Himmat that she started remembering him openly, without guilt. She continues to run Kargil Heights Filling Station as a tribute to her brave son.

Himmat Singh Shekhawat has made it his life's mission to help the families of fallen soldiers and share their stories with the world. Along with Shivaditay Modi, he is the founder of Rashtriya Riders, a biking group that pays tribute to the men and women in uniform. He is currently working with MakeMyTrip.